SID MEIER'S
CIVILIZATION III ®

Prima's Official Strategy Guide

David Ellis

Prima Games
A Division of Random House, Inc.

3000 Lava Ridge Court
Roseville, CA 95661
(916) 787-7000
www.primagames.com

SID MEIER'S CIVILIZATION III — PRIMA'S OFFICIAL STRATEGY GUIDE

Project Editor: Jill Hinckley
Editorial Assistant: Etelvina Hernandez
Product Manager: Sara E. Wilson

ISBN: 0-7615-3645-0

Library of Congress Catalog Card Number: 2001095679
Printed in the United States of America
01 02 03 04 DD 10 9 8 7 6 5 4 3 2 1

Contents

Acknowledgements

Writing a strategy guide is a collaborative effort, so I've got a lot of people to thank. First, thanks to the folks at Prima—Sara Wilson, Jill Hinckley, Teli Hernandez, and Asha Johnson for being so easy to work with and having the confidence in me to get it done under such a tight schedule. Also, thanks to the QA folks at Firaxis—Barry Caudill, Rex Martin, Jason Gleason, and Ellie Crawley—for providing me with pages of great tips that I would have never thought of on my own. The testers are always the most experienced players, and the book is much better thanks to their input. Also, a huge thanks goes to John Possidente, my intermediary with the development team, who made sure that information flowed smoothly and that I was always kept up to date on the latest changes.

Last, but *never* least, thanks to my wife, Meghan, who always supports me in whatever I do (and, as a *Civ* junkie, provided some helpful tips for the guide as well). Thanks, love!

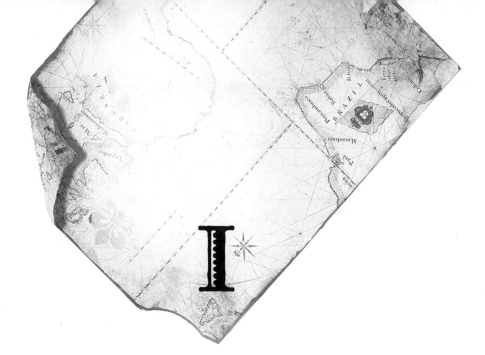

In the Beginning

In the 20-year history of computer games, arguably no game is better known and more admired than the *Sid Meier's Civilization®* game. Including the original game, which was released in 1992, there have been seven *Civilization®* products—five stand-alone games and two scenario collections. Millions of strategy gamers have lost countless hours of sleep pursing the perfect empire into the wee hours of the morning, ignoring the real world in favor of "just one more turn."

Now, just when you *Civ®* junkies have finally caught up on your shuteye, it's time to begin your empire building efforts anew. Kiss the spouse and kids goodbye, give the pets plenty of food, shut the door, and boot up your PC. It's time for *Civilization III*.

How to Use This Book

This guide introduces beginning and intermediate *Civ* players to the basic strategies of effective civilization growth and management. It also presents detailed information and statistics on every vital concept—information that can be used by veterans to develop new strategies and hone time-tested techniques so that they'll work with the many new rules and subtle changes that are present in *Civilization III*.

A step-by-step walkthrough is impossible—each *Civilization* game is different from the one before it. Play the tutorial game for a good game basics primer. Therein, you'll master the game mechanics and interface.

Civilization III relies on many interwoven concepts and activities, each of which has its own set of strategies. These concepts form a coherent game strategy that, while not ensuring victory, will certainly improve your chances of winning.

This book is divided into conceptual sections that mirror those of the game itself, and the concepts are discussed in roughly the order you'll deal with them.

- **Chapter I** goes over the basic differences between *Civilization III* and the previous *Civ* games.

- **Chapters II and III** deal with the decisions you make prior to building your first city, such as game setup options and the concepts of resources and terrain.

- **Chapter IV** deals with all of the issues involved in managing and maintaining your cities.

- **Chapter V** talks about empire management issues such as government, diplomacy, and trade.

- **Chapters VI, VII, and VIII** discuss the details of advances, improvements and Wonders, and units (respectively), plus all the concepts and strategies tied to them.

- **Chapter IX** offers general strategies for achieving each of the six victory conditions.

- **Chapter X** gives you the lowdown on the *Civilization III* editor and provides the basic information that advanced players need to customize the game to their hearts' content.

And, for those of you who like to know the "why" as well as the "how," the book ends with **Chapter XI,** an exclusive interview with *Civilization's* creator, game god Sid Meier, who provides some insight on the latest installment of one of the most popular game series of all time.

Read the guide from cover to cover or use it as a reference tome. Either way, the information you'll find here should help you in your quest to build an empire that stands the test of time.

WHAT'S NEW IN *CIVILIZATION III*?

The ultimate world building game is back with a vengeance. After giving us a taste in *Alpha Centauri* of the new ideas and features in *Civilization*, Sid Meier, Jeff Briggs, and the rest of the Firaxis team have gone back to basics, bringing *Civ* into the new millennium.

Civilization III, like its predecessors, has something for everyone. While the basic game remains much as veteran players remember it, the new features and rules throughout will delight—and sometimes confound—experienced world leaders.

The next few sections will give you an overview of the new features you can expect to encounter—and the old features that have gone the way of the Roman Empire.

Sweeping Changes

Most of the changes in *Civ III* are subtle and specific, but a few broad updates affect many facets of the game. The most prominent are:

- **Culture:** Every city now generates Culture Points based on its improvements and Wonders. Culture Points determine your civilization's sphere of influence—essentially, the borders of your empire. This means that your civilization isn't just an unconnected collection of city-states—it's a potentially contiguous empire. Chapters IV and V discuss Culture and its effects in more detail.

- **Barbarians:** Yes, you still have to deal with these marauding outsiders, but their activity has been subtly altered. No longer nameless hordes that materialize from the ether, they are named, minor tribes that operate from small villages that actually appear on the map. They are also unable to capture your cities, which gives you a little less to worry about. Discover the specifics of dealing with Barbarians in chapter VIII.

- **Civilization diversity:** The civilizations (usually referred to as "tribes" in the previous games) are no longer just different in name, temperament, and unit color. In *Civ III*, every civilization has game-specific advantages. Each civilization also has one unit that only

it can build. Chapter II talks more about the civilizations, and chapter VIII provides details on the civilization-specific units.

Terrain and Resources

Civ III incorporates a number of changes to the terrain and resources you rely on throughout the game. Terrain and resources are covered in detail in chapter III.

- **Special resource categories:** Special resources—Silk, Wine, Coal, Gold, and so on—are now divided into three categories: bonus, luxury, and strategic resources.

- **Resources tied to unit construction:** Some units cannot be built without access to certain strategic resources.

- **Fresh water irrigation:** Early in the game (prior to the discovery of Electricity), you can only build irrigation on terrain that has access to fresh water.

- **Colonies:** You can build colonies outside your empire to harvest strategic resources.

- **Better visibility:** Units can "see" farther when they're on top of hills and mountains.

- **Impassible terrain:** Some units are unable to move through certain terrain types. See the unit descriptions in chapter VIII for details.

Advances

Subtle changes in scientific research abound in *Civ III*. Veterans will recognize many of the advances from the previous games. Some technologies have been added, some have been renamed, and others have been removed altogether. See chapter VI for details on the science of *Civ III*.

NEW ADVANCES

Ecology	Nationalism
Education	Printing Press
Free Artistry	Satellites
Integrated Defense	Scientific Method
Military Tradition	Smart Weapons
Music Theory	Synthetic Fibers

Other scientific changes include:

- **Interactive research tree:** The science advisor screen now maps out the entire research tree for you. Use this tree to plan your research path and even to queue up multiple advances for future research.

- **Better-defined ages of civilization:** The four ages of civilization (Ancient Times, Middle Ages, Industrial Ages, and Modern Times) are now explicitly mapped out on the research tree.

Units and Combat

There have been quite a few changes in both military units themselves and in the way they interact. There are, of course, a number of new units available. Other units have been changed or abolished altogether. See chapter VIII for details.

NEW UNITS

Army	Musketmen
Cossack*	Nuclear Submarine
F-15*	Panzer*
Hoplite*	Radar Artillery
Immortals*	Rider*
Impi*	Samurai*
Jaguar Warrior*	Spearman
Leader	Swordsman
Longbowman	Tactical Nuke
Man-O-War*	War Chariot*
Modern Armor	War Elephant*
Mounted Warrior*	Worker

Civilization-specific unit

Additional unit and combat changes include:

- **Home cities eliminated:** Your units are now part of your empire as a whole rather than being attached to and supported from a single city.

- **The Gold standard:** Units are now supported strictly through the Gold in your treasury. No units in Civ III require food or shields for support.

- **Unit upgrades:** Obsolete units can now be upgraded to their modern equivalents— for a price, of course.

- **Settlers build only cities:** The new Worker unit handles all terrain improvement duties.

- **Bombardment:** Artillery units and ships now bombard targets rather than attacking them directly.

- **Capturing units:** Units with a zero defense no longer die when attacked. Instead, the attacking enemy instantly captures and takes control of them.

- **Leaders and Armies:** The new Leader unit can be used to group multiple units into a single, powerful Army unit.

City Improvements

As is true with advances and units, there have been additions, deletions, and changes to the improvements you can build in your cities.

NEW CITY IMPROVEMENTS
Hospital
SS Cockpit
SS Docking Bay
SS Planetary Party Lounge
SS Storage/Supply
SS Thrusters

Most of the city improvement changes are functional differences and new characteristics that improve and/or alter the function of the improvements. See chapter VII for details.

Wonders of the World

As with the city improvements, *Civ III*'s Wonders have gone through some functional renovation (and the occasional name change). This game also introduces Small Wonders—those that can be built by more than one civilization. For more details, check out chapter VII.

NEW WONDERS OF THE WORLD
Battlefield Medicine
Forbidden Palace
Heroic Epic
Intelligence Agency
Iron Works
Longevity
Military Academy
Strategic Missile Defense
The Pentagon
Wall Street

Interactions with Other Civilizations

Diplomacy and other interactions with your neighbors have been revised as well. More options are open to you now, and others have either disappeared or radically changed. Notable changes include:

- **More negotiation options:** During negotiations, you can trade many enticing things, from military treaties and maps, to vital resources, Workers, and cities.

- **No more Diplomats or Spies:** All of your espionage activities are now carried out through your embassies.

- **No more Caravans or Freight units:** Trade is now a function of connectivity via road, railroad, air, or sea. The trade units have been eliminated.

For more information on diplomacy and other civilization interactions, see chapter V.

More Ways to Win

In the previous *Civilization* games, you had two primary choices when it came to victory: build a spaceship and be the first to colonize Alpha Centauri or wipe all of your opponents off the face of the planet. You still have those options in *Civ III*, but you have other options as well.

- **Cultural Victory:** Win through Culture Points.

- **Diplomatic Victory:** Get elected to the head of the United Nations.

- **Domination Victory:** Win through territorial expansion.

- **Histographic Victory:** Win by having the highest Civilization Score.

Find a complete discussion of the various paths to victory in chapter IX.

Notable Exclusions

Knowing what has been added and updated is vital to formulating a sound strategy, but equally important are the concepts and rules that have been *removed*. Some of these will come as a welcome surprise to *Civ* veterans, while others will topple tried-and-true strategies used since the first game was released in 1992. The most salient deletions include:

- **Zones of Control:** You are no longer prevented from moving within one map square of an opposing unit or city. (Some units can still take certain liberties against others that pass through an adjacent square, though. See chapter VIII for details.)

- **Bribery:** It is no longer possible to bribe opposing units to join your army—and they can't bribe *your* units to join theirs. The only units that can be taken over by another civilization are Workers, who are traded in diplomatic negotiations, and units with a zero defense, which can be captured in combat.

- **Fundamentalism:** Sorry, warmongers. This form of government is history.

- **Automatic improvement sales:** Your cities no longer sell improvements without your permission when your treasury runs low. (At least, not on the easier difficulty levels.)

- **The Senate:** Remember how those guys were always going behind your back and making peace treaties during a nice, enjoyable war? Well, that's a thing of the past! Before you get too excited though, the Senate has been replaced by the concept of war weariness, which has similar effects. (See chapter V for details.)

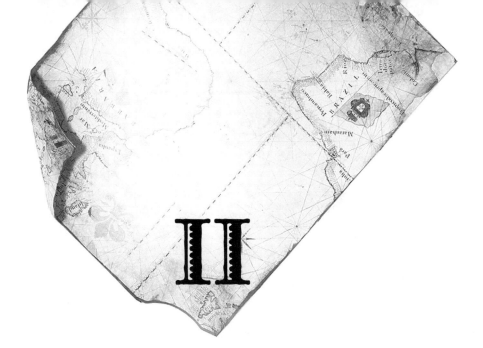

STARTING OFF ON THE RIGHT FOOT

xperienced players know that the decision-making processes in the *Civilization*® games begins before you build your first city. In fact, it begins before you even see the map!

Civilization III includes a wide variety of setup options that can radically affect how the game plays out. Depending on the options you select, each new game can be fundamentally different than the last.

This chapter talks about your up-front decisions, including world size and climate, difficulty level, level of competition, and tribe selection. By the end of the chapter, you'll know exactly how to set the options so that they best suit your preferred style of play.

CHOOSE YOUR WORLD

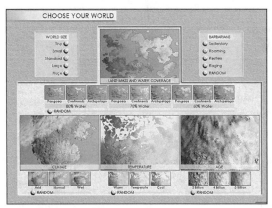

Choosing your world

The first set of options are primarily associated with the size, land/water composition, and weather. (Barbarian activity is covered

here as well.) These options greatly affect the level of conflict and the availability of resources in the game.

World Size

The size of the world determines the amount of terrain available for exploration— the larger the world, the more room there is to explore. Five world size options are available:

- Tiny (60x60 terrain squares)
- Small (80x80 terrain squares)
- Standard (100x100 terrain squares)
- Large (140x140 terrain squares)
- Huge (180x180 terrain squares)

Size *does* matter in *Civilization III*. When you play on a smaller world, the world map can be completely explored early in the game. Thus, you're likely to encounter most or all of your opponents very early on. Games on small worlds tend to be shorter because they usually degenerate into territorial squabbles that then turn into full-scale wars. Conquest Victories are the most common way to win in a small-world game.

Larger worlds lend themselves to a more leisurely game that revolves around prolonged exploration, peaceful expansion, and science-based victory. Depending on the number of opponents you select, you could be well into the Middle Ages or beyond before you encounter your neighbors. By that time you will have (hopefully) expanded to the point where your neighbors cannot easily bully you. If you prefer a peaceful strategy, large-world games are for you.

Land Mass and Water Coverage

Land mass and the ratio of water to land affect the game in a number of ways. The three land mass selections are:

- **Pangaea:** This world is dominated by one large interconnected landmass.
- **Continents:** Large bodies of water separate many large landmasses.
- **Archipelago:** Many small landmasses are scattered across a large, continuous body of water.

Land mass type greatly affects your strategy throughout the game. For example, on an Archipelago world, you have less room to explore on your starting continent. To grow your empire, you must take to the sea early and find new islands to conquer.

Your opponents are in the same boat (no pun intended) and, with all that exploring going on, you're bound to run into one another sooner than you might on a Continent world. Archipelago worlds foster a greater dependence on naval dominance.

Continents offer the most balanced game possibilities, though large continents are no guarantee against running into your neighbors early in the game. Starting positions are random, and you could end up next to a would-be conqueror on the first turn.

Pangaea worlds greatly reduce the need for naval units because everybody's on the same big continent. Ground and air units are the most useful here. On a big world, you usually have enough room to expand before you start running into your neighbors but, again, random chance might not operate in your favor.

NOTE

The Wonders of the World that affect every city on a continent—Hoover Dam, for example—tend to be more effective on worlds with large land masses. You can fit more cities on a large land mass.

In addition to land mass choices, you can set the amount of water on the world. This determines the ratio of land tiles to water tiles. The more land you have, the less likely that you'll be fighting with your neighbors early in the game to take advantage of the limited resources.

NOTE

If you want to play on an Earth-like world, stick to the defaults for land mass and water coverage: 70 percent water with Continents.

Climate

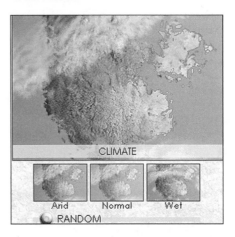

The amount of available moisture affects the availability of certain terrain types, which, in turn, affects your food production and city growth possibilities. Your choices are:

- **Arid:** A dry world has an abundance of dry terrain types, such as Plains and Deserts.

- **Normal:** This world has an average distribution of all terrain types.

- **Wet:** A rainy world has an abundance of wet terrain types such as Flood Plains and Swamps, and a greater-than-normal occurrence of rivers.

Empire growth can be difficult in either of the extremes. Arid climates don't lend themselves well to food output, which means slow city growth. Wet climates and their attendant terrain types, while abundant food producers, are less conducive to commerce. Disease also plagues wet worlds, making it difficult to keep your cities growing.

The Normal climate, with its even mix of terrain types, is the easiest to deal with. (For more information on terrain types, see chapter III.)

Temperature

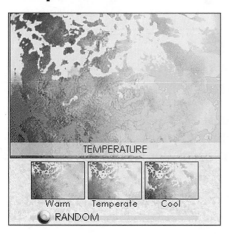

Temperature also affects the available terrain types. Your choices are:

- **Warm:** This climate has few Tundra squares but a higher number of Desert and Jungle squares.

- **Temperate:** This climate is similar to Earth's, with an even mixture of "hot" and "cold" terrain types.

- **Cool:** This climate has a larger number of Tundra squares but fewer Deserts and Jungles.

Once again, moderation is the key to an easier game. At either temperature extreme, you're bound to run into more undesirable terrain than you'd like. Both Desert and Tundra are extremely difficult to deal with in terms of resource production. If you don't want that headache, stick to the Temperate setting. Play on a Warm or Cool world only if you're looking for a challenge.

Age

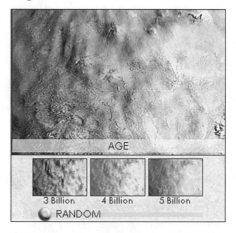

The Age option affects not only the frequency of occurrence for certain terrain types, but their distribution on the map as well. The Age choices are:

- **3 Billion:** In a young world, Mountains are more prevalent than Hills, and large tracts of similar terrain types occur together.

- **4 Billion:** In a world of average age, average terrain distribution broken up by occasional tracts of like terrain.

- **5 Billion:** In an old world, Hills are more prevalent than Mountains and like terrain type tends to vary widely over short distances.

Age can have a profound effect on city growth throughout the game. A well-balanced city needs a variety of resources to prosper—a good balance of food, shields, and commerce. On young planets, with their huge swathes of similar terrain, such a balance can be hard to find at any given site. In fact, city sites can be at a premium if you start the game in the middle of a mass of unfriendly terrain such as Desert or Jungle. The unpredictable terrain distribution on an old world can be almost as bad. Again, stick to the default unless you're looking for a challenge.

> **NOTE**
> Except for World Size, all of the world customization options can be set to Random. This adds an unpredictable edge to every game.

Barbarians

Those pesky Barbarians—you can't live with them, and you can't live without them. What you *can* do, however, is set their activity to a level that you're comfortable with. Your choices are:

- **Sedentary:** This is the closest you can come to turning the Barbarians off. This restricts their activity to their villages, where they can do you no harm (unless you seek them out).

- **Roaming:** Barbarian villages appear from time to time, but with low frequency, throughout the game. Expect infrequent Barbarian incursions at this setting.

- **Restless:** Barbarian villages pop up with greater frequency and produce more Barbarians. Attacks are more of a nuisance at this level.

- **Raging:** Barbarian villages appear quite frequently and produce enough Barbarians to pose a serious threat to nearby cities. At this level, seek out and destroy the Barbarian village as soon as the Barbarians rear their ugly heads.

- **Random:** Add some excitement to the game! You won't know how bad the Barbarian problem is until they're swarming all over you.

At anything but "Raging" level, Barbarians in *Civ® III* aren't that difficult to deal with, especially on the lower difficulty levels. In fact, having them pop up with moderate frequency tends to fatten your

treasury—you get a reward every time you take out one of their villages.

For more information on dealing with Barbarians, see chapter VIII.

PLAYER SETUP

The Player Setup screen

After you've got your world squared away, it's time to select your civilization, opponents, rules, and game difficulty. While many of these options and their effects are pretty obvious—especially to *Civ* veterans—*Civilization III* adds several new features and twists to the game that are worth noting.

Your Civilization/ Your Opponents

One of the biggest changes in *Civilization III* is greater differentiation between the various civilizations. Instead of simply having different faces and different general game-play attitudes and habits, tribal differences now include differing philosophies, special advantages, different combinations of starting advances, and even one civilization-specific unit that only that civilization can build. (Civilization-specific units are described in detail in chapter VIII.)

Tables 2-1 and 2-2 summarizes the abilities and characteristics of the 16 civilizations in the game.

TABLE 2-1. CIVILIZATION CHARACTERISTICS

CIVILIZATION	COMMERCIAL	EXPANSIONIST	INDUSTRIOUS	MILITARISTIC	RELIGIOUS	SCIENTIFIC
Americans		X	X			
Aztecs				X	X	
Babylonians					X	X
Chinese			X	X		
Egyptians			X		X	
English	X	X				
French	X		X			
Germans	X	X				
Greeks	X					X
Indians	X				X	
Iroquois		X			X	
Japanese				X	X	
Persians			X			X
Romans	X			X		
Russians		X				X
Zulus		X		X		

TABLE 2-2. BONUSES BASED ON CHARACTERISTICS

CHARACTERISTIC	STARTING ADVANCE	SPECIAL EFFECT 1	SPECIAL EFFECT 2
Commercial	Alphabet	Extra commerce in city square	Lower corruption
Expansionist	Pottery	Better booty from villages	Starts game with a Scout
Industrious	Masonry	Workers work faster	Extra shield in city square
Militaristic	Warrior Code or The Wheel	Reduced military improvement costs	Unit promotions more likely
Religious	Ceremonial Burial	Reduced religious improvement costs	No Anarchy between governments
Scientific	Bronze Working	Free random advance at the start of each era	Reduced science improvement costs

As you can see, choosing your civilization is now more than just a matter of choosing which unit color and leader image you like the best. This decision now determines important factors that affect the course of your entire game!

Choose your civilization based on your preferred style of play. Although a savvy player can match any civilization to any style of play with some degree of success, certain civilizations lend themselves better to achieving certain victory paths. Here are some guidelines:

- **Domination Victory:** Americans, Chinese, English, Germans, Iroquois, Russians, Zulus
- **Diplomatic Victory:** Aztecs, Babylonians, Chinese, Egyptians, Greeks, Indians, Iroquois, Japanese, Russians
- **Cultural Victory:** Aztecs, Babylonians, Egyptians, English, French, Germans, Greeks, Indians, Iroquois, Japanese, Romans
- **Conquest Victory:** Aztecs, Japanese, Persians Romans, Zulus
- **Space Victory:** Americans, Babylonians, Egyptians, French, Greeks, Persians, Russians

Of course, the civilization-specific characteristics apply to your computer opponents as well. *Civilization III* allows you to select the opponents you want to play against—the larger the world, the more opponents you can choose. If you don't select any, the computer picks the number and identity of your opponents at random. If you want to know what you're up against, pick them yourself. Otherwise, anything goes.

RULES

The rules and their implications are explained in detail in the game manual, so there's no point in belaboring them here. Basically, the game allows you to deactivate victory conditions. Doing so makes the game harder to win because your paths to victory are limited. You can also deactivate the civilization-specific characteristics and units.

NOTE

If you long for the good old days, use the Rules section of the Player Setup screen to approximate the original *Civilization* experience. Turn off "Allow Civ-Specific Abilities" and all of the victory options except "Space" and "Military." There are still differences, of course, but this is as close as you can get. Enjoy!

Difficulty

No game would be complete without the ability to adjust the gameplay to make it painfully easy or excruciatingly difficult. That's where the game difficulty settings come in. Veteran players will immediately recognize the six difficulty settings, which range from Chieftain (easiest) to Deity (most difficult).

Table 2-3 shows how difficulty level affects the game. The game features and statistics listed in the table are as follows:

- **Content Citizens:** The number of citizens in each city that are "born" content. All citizens added after this number are automatically unhappy. (See chapter IV for details.)

- **Opponent Build/Advance Rate:** A multiplier that determines how fast your opponents build units, improvements, Wonders, and complete research compared to you. For example, if this number is 200 percent, your opponents take twice as long as you to complete these tasks.

- **Barbarian Combat Bonus:** This multiplier is added to your units' stats when they fight Barbarian units.

TABLE 2-3. EFFECTS OF DIFFICULTY LEVEL

GAME FEATURES	CHIEFTAIN	WARLORD	PRINCE	KING	EMPEROR	DEITY
Content Citizens	4	3	2	2	1	1
Opponent Build/Advance Rate	200%	120%	100%	90%	80%	60%
Barbarian Combat Bonus	+400%	+200%	+100%	+50%	+25%	+0%

There are also a number of general difficulty effects:

- On Chieftain and Warlord levels, units do not automatically disband when you run out of Gold to support them.

- On Chieftain and Warlord levels, improvements aren't automatically sold off when you run out of Gold to maintain them.

- On all levels, your first few units require no support. On Chieftain and Warlord levels, several additional units are support-free.

- Corruption increases with difficulty level.

- The lower the difficulty level, the more likely it is that you'll receive a reward of some sort when you visit a village (goodie hut).

- Your opponents are more lenient during negotiations at lower difficulty levels.

- Your opponents are less aggressive and less likely to break treaties at lower levels.

- In all other situations (those not listed here or in Table 2-3), your opponents play at Prince level.

> **NOTE**
> Game difficulty level no longer affects the amount of money you start with. You start with 10 Gold in your treasury regardless of difficulty level.

WHAT OPTIONS ARE RIGHT FOR YOU?

Hitting the right combination of game options is the key to getting the best possible game experience for your level of expertise. Although the potential options combinations are endless, here are a few general guidelines for setting up a game that's right for you.

For a long, laid-back, non-confrontational game:

- **World Size:** Huge
- **Land mass and Water Coverage:** Continents, 60 percent water
- **Climate:** Normal
- **Temperature:** Temperate
- **Age:** 4 Billion
- **Opponents:** 2–4; anyone non-militaristic and non-expansionist

For a fast and furious military confrontation:

- **World Size:** Tiny
- **Land mass and Water Coverage:** Pangaea, 80 percent water
- **Climate:** Arid or Wet
- **Temperature:** Warm or Cool

- **Age:** 3 Billion
- **Opponents:** 7; Aztecs, Romans, Persians, Zulus, Japanese, English, Germans

For a Cultural free-for-all:

- **World Size:** Standard
- **Land mass and Water Coverage:** Pangaea, 80 percent water
- **Climate:** Normal
- **Temperature:** Temperate
- **Age:** 4 Billion
- **Opponents:** 4–7; choose from Aztecs, Iroquois, Egyptians, Babylonians, Indians, Japanese, French, Greeks

For a challenging, all-out race to Alpha Centauri:

- **World Size:** Huge
- **Land mass and Water Coverage:** Continents, 60 percent water
- **Climate:** Normal
- **Temperature:** Temperate
- **Age:** 4 Billion
- **Opponents:** 2–7; choose from Americans, Russians, French, Greeks, Romans, Egyptians, Babylonians, Chinese

III

RESOURCES AND CITY CONSTRUCTION

Now that you've selected your civilization and the general conditions of the game and game world, it's time to start building your empire. Your first task is to build your empire's capital city. But where should you build it? This decision, made when your empire is no more than a few fledgling units, is easily as important as any you'll make in the game.

The last section of the chapter discusses selecting your first city site and improving the surrounding terrain so that you can get your empire off to a strong start. We'll begin, however, with an in-depth look at the resources you'll be most concerned

with throughout the game—food, shields, and commerce—as well as a detailed look at the new ap resource model in the *Civilization® III* game.

RESOURCES AND TERRAIN

Throughout the game, you build and acquire cities. The location of these cities defines their fate throughout the game. A well-placed city grows briskly and has rapid production. A poorly placed city stagnates, growing slowly and producing units and improvements at a snail's pace.

To build cities that prosper, you need to understand the game's resources and their effect on your empire.

The "Big Three"

Although there are a dozen different terrain types and more than 20 bonus, luxury, and strategic resources in *Civilization III*, everything comes down to three basic components, the stuff of which empires are made: food, shields, and commerce. Every terrain type produces these three major resources in different combinations.

Food

 Food serves two roles in *Civilization III*. First, it keeps the city's population alive. Every turn, each citizen in the city consumes two units of food. So, in a size 10 city, that's 20 units per turn. If the surrounding terrain isn't producing enough food to meet the population's needs, food is drawn from the city's reserves (the food storage box). When the food storage box is empty, people start dying—one per turn until the food deficit is corrected.

The other function food serves is population growth. Each turn, any food not consumed by the city population is placed in the food storage box. When the box fills up, the city's population increases by one. The greater your food production, the faster your city grows. (See the game manual for more details.) So, by locating

your cities in areas where the terrain produces abundant food, you increase the city's potential for rapid growth.

> **NOTE**
>
> In previous *Civilization* games, food served a third purpose—it supported Settler units in the field. Unit support in *Civilization III* is paid in Gold for all units. Food is never used for unit support.

Shields

 Shields represent raw materials. Your cities use them to produce units, improvements, and Wonders of the World. All the shields collected by the city each turn are placed in the production box, where they are applied to the city's current production project. When enough shields are accumulated to cover the price of the unit, improvement, or Wonder being produced, that item is completed and the city can go on to produce something else. The more shield-producing terrain that surrounds your cities, the faster your cities can produce things.

> **NOTE**
>
> Prior to *Civilization III*, shields supported a city's units. Now, all shields are used for production and unit support is paid in Gold from the central treasury.

Commerce

 Commerce, which was known as "Trade" in previous *Civilization* games, is the most complicated of the three major resources. The commerce a city produces is divided three ways:

- Science

- Taxes

- Entertainment

Although the principles of commerce in *Civ® III* are pretty much the same as those in the previous games, veterans should note some subtle changes.

The City Display now shows only two of the three commerce categories—science and taxes. The top line shows the percentage of commerce allocated to taxes—unit support, improvement maintenance, and (if there's anything left) your treasury. The bottom shows the percentage of commerce allocated to science—researching new civilization advances.

The commerce breakdown on the City Display.

The third component, entertainment, is now monitored and controlled from the Domestic Advisor's screen. The two sliders represent science (top) and entertainment (bottom).

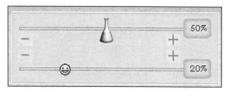

The science and entertainment sliders on the Domestic Advisor's screen.

On either screen you can see the commerce percentage allocated to two of the three commerce categories. The difference in the percentages is the amount of commerce allocated to the third category. So, if the commerce bars on the City Display show 60 percent taxes and 30 percent science, the remaining 10 percent is allocated to entertainment.

Each commerce component is important in its own way:

- **Taxes:** Taxes take on a new level of importance in *Civilization III*. They now maintain city improvements and all of your units. The taxes generated by your cities are combined and all improvement, unit maintenance, and support is subtracted from the total. The remaining Gold (if any) is placed in your treasury.

- **Science:** This is, arguably, the most important facet of commerce. Science is used to research new civilization advances. As discussed in chapter VI, every advance has a research "cost" that must be paid before it can be discovered. Every turn, the portion of commerce allocated to science is applied to the

current research project. The more commerce you allocate to science, the faster the advance is discovered.

- **Entertainment:** This is commerce that is channeled into making the city's residents happy. Entertainment is added to any luxuries produced by terrain, and "happy faces" produced by city improvements and Wonders in the city, determining the disposition of your population. The more entertainment your people have, the happier they are.

Chapter IV goes into the finer details of optimizing your commerce and how each of the three facets of this important resource figure into the successful operation of your cities.

The Lay of the Land

Now that you understand the three basic building blocks of *Civilization* survival, take a look at where they come from—the terrain itself. There are 12 basic terrain types, each with its own set of characteristics and resource ratios. There are also 22 special resources divided into three different categories: bonus resources, luxury resources, and strategic resources.

The next few sections look at all of these features in detail.

Basic Terrain Types

The world map is divided into hundreds of individual squares, each of which is assigned one of 12 basic terrain types. Each terrain type produces a different combination of food, shields, and commerce each turn. Different terrain types also affect unit movement and line of sight, as well as several other subtle aspects of gameplay.

> **NOTE**
>
> Veteran players should note that the Glacier terrain from *Civ II* (which was known as Arctic terrain in the original game) is nowhere to be found in *Civilization III*.

Table 3-1 lists the following vital statistics for each terrain type:

- **Food/Shields/Commerce:** The combination of "big three" resources produced by the terrain. For example, a terrain type that shows 0/1/0 in this category produces no food, one shield, and no commerce each turn.

- **Move Cost:** The base number of points a unit must expend to move into the terrain square.

- **Defensive Bonus:** The bonus applied to a unit's defense statistic when the unit occupies the terrain square.

- **Irrigation Bonus:** The resource bonus received when the terrain is improved through irrigation.

- **Mining Bonus:** The resource bonus received when the terrain is improved through mining.

- **Road Bonus:** The resource bonus received when a road is built in the terrain square. (In addition to this bonus, roads always decrease the movement cost of any terrain square to 1/3.)

TABLE 3-1. TERRAIN RESOURCES

TERRAIN TYPE	FOOD/SHIELDS/ COMMERCE	MOVE COST	DEFENSIVE BONUS	IRRIGATION BONUS	MINING BONUS	ROAD BONUS
Coast	1/0/2	1	+10%	—	—	—
Desert	0/1/0	1	+10%	+1 food	+1 shield	+1 commerce
Flood Plain	3/0/0	1	+10%	+1 food	—	+1 commerce
Forest	1/2/0	2	+25%	—	—	+1 commerce
Grassland	2/0/0	1	+10%	+1 food	+1 shield	+1 commerce
Hills	1/1/0	2	+50%	—	+2 shields	+1 commerce
Jungle	1/0/0	3	+25%	—	—	+1 commerce
Mountains	0/1/0	3	+100%	—	+2 shields	+1 commerce
Ocean	1/0/0	1	+10%	—	—	—
Plains	1/1/0	1	+10%	+1 food	+1 shield	+1 commerce
Sea	1/0/1	1	+10%	—	—	—
Tundra	1/0/0	1	+10%	—	+1 shield	+1 commerce

Coast

In the previous *Civilization* games, large bodies of water were entirely composed of Ocean squares. In *Civ III*, that one terrain type has been split into three: Coast, Ocean, and Sea. Coast squares are land/water squares that border a large body of water.

These squares have good commerce and provide food. Occasionally, you'll find Coast squares with the Fish bonus resource. Coastal cities built near these resources tend to grow quickly because of the additional food the Fish provide.

NOTE

The inland "seas" in *Civilization III* are usually made up exclusively of Coast terrain.

Desert

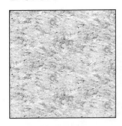

Avoid building cities in areas surrounded by Desert, and under no circumstances should you ever build a city *on* a Desert square. The only possible reason for building near a Desert is to gamble on the presence of Oil, an important strategic resource. Even so, never include more than one or two Desert squares within your city radius—if you do, you run the risk of slow growth and starvation in that city.

Flood Plain

Flood Plains are new to *Civilization III*. They provide more food than any other

terrain type—that means fast city growth in cities surrounded by Flood Plains.

There is one drawback, however. Flood Plains breed disease. When one

of your citizens is working a Flood Plains square, there is a chance each turn that disease will strike the city, reducing its population. Even so, disease strikes infrequently enough that it's worth the risk for the extra food.

NOTE

When you build a city on a terrain type that produces no shields and cannot normally be upgraded to make it produce shields, the game automatically provides the city square with a shield production of one per turn.

Forest

Forests have always been wonderful assets to a city. They provide the most shields of any terrain type while still providing food. In *Civilization III*, Forests offer an additional bonus—they can be harvested for a one-time windfall of 10 shields. This is a great way to hurry the production of an important unit, improvement, or Wonder.

Because Forests produce only one food per turn, a city built on a Forest square grows at a slower-than-normal rate—but it benefits from the Forest's defensive bonus. Although you shouldn't make a habit of building your cities in Forests, such a city can be successful if the surrounding squares produce enough food to compensate.

Grassland

Grasslands are one of the two most versatile terrain sites, along with Plains. Each has its indigenous advantage. In this case, it's food. The Grassland's high food output

(which is further increased with irrigation) ensures fast city growth. Grasslands make decent city sites.

There are two types of Grassland squares— standard Grassland and enhanced Grassland. They look identical except that enhanced Grassland has a small blue-white dot in the center. Enhanced Grassland squares produce one additional shield.

> **TIP**
>
> *When you have a choice between building your city on a Grassland square or a nearby enhanced Grassland square, choose the standard Grassland as your city site. That way, you'll get the "free" shield in the city square (see note earlier in this chapter) and can still exploit the bonus shield in the enhanced Grassland square.*

Hills

Because of the number of shields that Hills produce when they're mined, building your cities near at least one Hill is a good idea. Hills are also better than Mountains in that they they produce food as well as shields, making them more versatile. Hills are also home to a large number of special resources.

Cities built on Hills suffer the same slow growth as those built on any other terrain type whose food production cannot be improved. However, hilltop cities enjoy a considerable defensive bonus. If you build on a Hill, make sure the surrounding terrain can produce enough food to promote and sustain the city's growth.

Jungle

Jungles are inhospitable places, and their usefulness is limited. They cannot be improved (except with roads), and they produce only a single food unit each turn. On top of all that, they can introduce disease into your city (just like Flood Plains). *Never* build a city in a Jungle square. Never.

The only advantage of Jungles is that they sometimes house Rubber—a strategic resource that becomes very important in the later stages of the game—as well as a variety of luxury resources. Only if one of these is present should you even consider building a city with a Jungle in its radius.

> **TIP**
>
> *When you want to reap the benefits of a special resource but, for some reason, you don't want the terrain square that contains the resource inside your city radius, consider having a Worker build a road to it and set up a colony to harvest the resource.*

Mountains

Like Jungles, Mountains are entirely unsuitable as city sites. Even the massive defensive bonus your units receive in this terrain doesn't compensate for the total lack of food there.

Mountains are an excellent source of some of the most important strategic resources in the game, including Iron, Saltpeter, and Aluminum. As such, it's useful to include mountains inside some of your cities' radii.

Ocean

Ocean is the deep water that appears three squares and farther off the coast. Most of the Ocean squares on larger worlds or worlds where land is sparse will go unused. However, one or more Ocean squares usually fall within the city radius of each coastal city.

When possible, choose city sites where the Ocean square(s) house a special resource, such as Fish or (better still) Whales. These resource-enhanced Ocean squares are a vast improvement over the standard variety.

Plains

Plains are arguably the best city sites, especially early in the game. Cities built on Plains generate slightly less food than Grassland cities, which makes them grow a little slower. This keeps unhappiness at bay a little longer—a real boon on the higher difficulty levels. Plains make up for this by offering a shield—something that Grasslands lack.

TIP

When you build a city, the terrain square on which you build it is automatically improved in every way possible: irrigation, mining, and roads. That means that the city square itself reaps the increased benefits of the improved terrain. This makes the choice of terrain for a city very important. Cities built on terrain that cannot benefit from one or more terrain improvement method will accumulate fewer resources than those built on highly improvable terrain.

Sea

This intermediate water terrain falls along the shoreline, between Coast squares and Ocean squares. Every coastal city includes at least one Sea square in its city radius.

Sea squares are just like Coast squares except that they produce one less commerce. As with Ocean and Coast squares, Sea terrain is most valuable if it contains a special resource—in this case, Whales or Fish.

Tundra

Tundra is essentially a Jungle without the disease, though it *is* slightly more improvable. As is true of most of the inhospitable terrain types, several special resources that appear in Tundra squares are worth having. Your best bet in this case is to set up a colony. Don't include Tundra within your city radius unless you absolutely have to, and *never* build a city on a Tundra square.

Special Resources

Scattered around the world are enhanced terrain squares that produce additional resources. In *Civilization III*, special resources are divided into three categories, each of which provides a set of unique benefits.

Bonus Resources

Bonus resources increase the productivity of normal terrain. Their presence causes a terrain square to produce more food, shields, and/or commerce than it normally would. Cities built with bonus resources inside their city radius tend to be more successful. For instance, a city with one or more Wheat squares inside its city radius has more food production potential and grows faster as a result.

Table 3-2 lists all of the bonus resources, their effects on food, shield, and commerce production, and the terrain types on which they are found.

TABLE 3-2. EFFECTS OF BONUS RESOURCES

RESOURCE	FOOD	SHIELDS	COMMERCE	TERRAIN TYPES
Cattle	+2	+1	+0	Grasslands, Plains, Tundra
Fish	+2	+0	+1	Coast, Sea, Ocean
Game	+1	+0	+0	Tundra, Forest, Jungle
Gold	+0	+0	+4	Hills, Mountains
Whales	+1	+1	+2	Sea, Ocean
Wheat	+2	+0	+0	Flood Plains, Grasslands, Plains

NOTE

Changing the terrain on a square containing special resources does not remove or change the special resource. For example, when you harvest a Forest that contains Game, the Game remains even when the Forest is changed to Plains.

Luxury Resources

Luxury resources improve terrain in the same manner as bonus resources—they allow the terrain square to produce additional basic resources (usually commerce). Luxury resources also help keep your population happy. Every luxury resource to which the city has access has the potential to make one content citizen happy.

NOTE

To reap the happiness benefit of a luxury resource, you must build a road to it. You don't have to have a citizen working on the terrain square to reap the happiness benefits of the luxury, nor does the luxury have to be within the city radius. To collect the food, shield, and commerce bonuses, however, the terrain must be within your city radius and one of your citizens must be working on it.

Unlike bonus resources, luxury resources can be traded between your cities and with your opponents. (See chapter V for more information on trading.)

Table 3-3 lists all of the luxury resources, their effects on food, shield, and commerce production, and the terrain types on which they are found.

TABLE 3-3.
EFFECTS OF LUXURY RESOURCES

RESOURCE	FOOD	SHIELDS	COMMERCE	TERRAIN TYPES
Dyes	+0	+0	+1	Forest, Jungle
Furs	+0	+1	+1	Tundra
Gems	+0	+0	+4	Mountains
Incense	+0	+0	+1	Hills, Desert
Ivory	+0	+0	+2	Forest, Plains
Silks	+0	+0	+3	Forest
Spices	+0	+0	+2	Forest, Jungle
Wines	+1	+0	+1	Grasslands, Hills

Strategic Resources

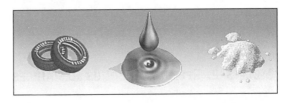

Strategic resources are, without a doubt, the most important of the special resource types. Like luxury resources, they provide an increase in basic resources that the terrain they occupy produces (sometimes shields, sometimes commerce, but never food). They can also be traded between your connected cities and between your civilization and others.

What makes strategic resources so vital is that certain units, improvements, and Wonders of the World—not to mention railroads—require that you have access to specific strategic resources before you can build them. If you don't have access to the resource, you can't produce the item in question.

Strategic resources are not all visible at the start of the game. Instead, they appear as your research advances. Even so, it's possible to plan your city sites to take advantage of these resources when they do appear by noting the type of terrain where they can exist.

CAUTION

Strategic resources that are connected to any civilization's trade network have a chance of disappearing every turn. This represents the depletion of the resource. The chance of resource depletion is always low (never more than 1% per turn), but don't be surprised if your valuable resource stash suddenly vanishes. Uranium and Oil are the most prone to depletion, but Iron, Saltpeter, Aluminum, and Coal supplies can also run out.

Table 3-4 lists all of the strategic resources, their effects on food, shield, and commerce production, and the terrain types on which they are found. Also listed is the civilization advance that you must discover before the resource appears.

TABLE 3-4. EFFECTS OF STRATEGIC RESOURCES

RESOURCE	FOOD	SHIELDS	COMMERCE	TERRAIN TYPES	APPEARS AFTER
Aluminum	+0	+2	+0	Desert, Hills, Mountains, Plains	Rocketry
Coal	+0	+2	+1	Hills, Jungles, Mountains	Steam Power
Horses	+0	+0	+1	Grasslands, Hills, Plains	The Wheel
Iron	+0	+1	+0	Hills, Mountains	Iron Working
Oil	+0	+1	+2	Desert, Plains, Tundra	Refining
Rubber	+0	+0	+2	Forests, Jungles	Replaceable Parts
Saltpeter	+0	+0	+1	Deserts, Hills, Mountains, Tundra	Gunpowder
Uranium	+0	+2	+3	Forests, Mountains	Fission

Rivers

As in *Civilization II*, *Civ III* doesn't treat rivers as distinct terrain types. Instead, they are a terrain feature that appears in many different terrain types. In fact, they actually flow *between* terrain squares in this game.

Rivers provide the following benefits:

- +1 commerce to the terrain squares they border.

- A fresh water source for irrigation of adjacent squares.

- A 50 percent defensive bonus for a defending unit that is attacked across a river.

- Movement between two terrain squares divided by a river costs only 1/3 of a movement point (*after* you discover Engineering).

- Any city that includes a river inside the city radius can build a Hydro Plant and/or the Hoover Dam Wonder of the World.

- Any city that includes a river inside the city radius can build a Nuclear Plant.

Villages

Scattered across the world early in the game are many small villages that house

minor tribes. These villages, often referred to as "goodie huts" by *Civ* veterans, belong to no one—at least, they don't belong to your *opponents*. Moving one of your units into a village often provides you with a reward.

The possible results of entering a village are as follows:

- **The village is deserted:** You receive nothing for entering.

- **The villagers attack:** One or more hostile Barbarian units appear and attack your unit.

- **Gold:** You receive a gift of Gold from the villagers.

- **Advance:** The villagers impart their ancient wisdom to you in the form of a new civilization advance.

- **Military unit:** The villagers create a military unit that joins your civilization.

- **Settler:** The nomadic villagers join your civilization in the form of a Settler unit.

- **New city:** The villagers are so impressed with your civilization that they form a new city that becomes a part of your empire.

Because the positive results of exploring villages far outweigh the negative, *always* visit every village you come across. When possible, enter the village with a military unit (as opposed to a Settler or a Worker) to prevent the certain loss of a valuable unit should the results of your visit be hostile.

NOTE

In *Civilization II*, village contents were randomly generated at the moment you visited them. This allowed you to save the game prior to visiting the village and keep reloading the game until you got the results you wanted. *This is no longer the case.*

BUILDING CITIES AND OPTIMIZING TERRAIN

Even with the addition of culture and empire borders, your civilization is at heart just a collection of individual cities. By building effective cities that thrive and grow, you create a prosperous, growing empire.

The remainder of this chapter focuses on selecting the right locations for your cities and optimizing the surrounding terrain to ensure that your cities prosper.

Location, Location, Location

Armed with the terrain knowledge you gained earlier in this chapter, you should be ready to build a city. The site you select for each city determines whether the city will thrive or stagnate.

As explained in the game manual, every city generates resources by putting its citizens to work in the city radius, the 20 squares surrounding the city square itself. Every time a city's population increases, the new citizen is automatically put to work on one of the terrain squares inside the city radius. You can see the type and number of resources generated in each terrain square by checking out the resource map on the City Display.

The resource map of an established city.

As you can see, the surrounding terrain squares, as well as the city square itself, produce resources. The city square maximizes resource production by automatically establishing all of the possible terrain improvements—irrigation, mining, and roads—when it is built. For example, a city built on a Plains square receives the normal one food and one shield provided by Plains, plus an additional unit of food (for irrigation) and one unit of commerce (for roads).

NOTE

You receive the irrigation bonus regardless of whether the city is adjacent to a water source. However, the irrigation in the city cannot be used as a water source for irrigating surrounding terrain squares.

In addition to picking an optimum square on which to build the city, look at the surrounding terrain. Most terrain types can be improved through irrigation and mining, but that takes time. If your city site isn't surrounded by a good balance of resources, the city will stagnate and become a burden on your empire.

Choosing a proper location for your first city is one of the most critical decisions you'll make. Nowhere in the game is it easier to fall behind your opponents than right at the beginning, when everyone's resources are limited and your empires are small. If your first city doesn't grow, can't produce units and improvements quickly, and can't generate enough commerce to keep the research effort going, your game is likely to be short.

Build your first city on a square that produces at least one of each resource— food, shields, and commerce. (Remember to take the automatic terrain enhancements in the city square into account.) Balance growth versus production by choosing a site that produces either more food or more shields.

As for the surrounding terrain, make sure that the nearby resources compliment each other. Shield-rich Hills and Forests should be balanced by big food producers such as Grasslands and Flood Plains. Always be on the lookout for special resources, especially luxury resources that can enhance your population's happiness and be traded to induce happiness in other cities as well. As your technology progresses, watch for the strategic resources you'll need to complete pivotal units, improvements, and Wonders. Rivers, with their added commerce, are a boon as well. Build near them if possible.

Finally, if you are near the coastline, consider building a coastal city. Ships can be built in coastal cities only, and the added ability to explore the world via the ocean is a great aid in the rapid expansion of your empire.

By following these basic guidelines, your first city and, indeed, all of your cities, should prosper. There is more leeway later in the game to build cities on less-than-perfect sites, as an established empire can support one or two slow-growing cities with little problem. However, unless there's a strategic reason not to do so, choose the best location possible for every city.

TIP

One of the biggest debates between Civ players is not where to build the first city but when to build it. Many believe that you should build your city on the first turn in the square where you start the game. Their reasoning is that the sooner the first city is built, the sooner research and unit production can begin.

Others feel it's best to take your time—and we happen to agree. It often pays to use your Worker and Settler to explore the area for a couple of turns to see if there's a better potential city site nearby. Although this might put you a turn or two behind your opponents in research, the long-term benefits could be great. Wouldn't it be a shame to build on a mediocre site only to find a resource-rich site just a few squares away?

Increasing Resource Yield

As a city's population grows, resource production increases. Every new citizen means one more square within the city radius is producing resources for you. Eventually, however, the natural resource production for each square just isn't enough. Luckily, there are a number of ways to increase resource production.

Terrain Improvements

The easiest way to increase a city's resource yield is to improve the surrounding terrain. Your Workers can do this in a number of ways:

- **Irrigation:** Increases food production by one unit of food per turn in Flood Plains, Grasslands, Plains, and Deserts.

- **Mining:** Increases shield production in Grasslands, Plains, Deserts, and Tundra by one shield per turn, and in Hills and Mountains by two shields per turn.

- **Roads/Railroads:** Increases commerce in all non-water terrain types by one per turn.

- **Harvesting Forests:** Provides the city with a one-time bonus of 10 shields and converts the Forest into Plains.

Workforce Adjustments

New members of your population are automatically put to work when a city grows—but they don't always end up on the terrain square where you want them.

The game tries to anticipate your needs when it puts your people to work, but you might not always agree with its choices. Also, situations might arise from time to time that necessitate the production of one particular resource over another. Make these adjustments by moving your citizens to terrain squares that produce more of the required resource.

Suppose you wanted to stimulate shield production so you could finish an improvement quickly. Consider the city shown in the figure below. Although the city is doing well enough, its shield output is fairly low.

A city with low shield output.

Now, look at the next figure. By simply moving the workers from the Coastal and Sea squares to Forest, Plains, and Grassland squares, shield output has more than doubled.

The same city, with its shield output greatly improved.

Although the game generally does a good job at balancing your workforce to output a good mix of resources, breeze through your city screens from time to time to make sure resource output levels meet your current needs.

Improvements and Wonders

Certain improvements and Wonders of the World can increase food, shield, and commerce production in your cities—some locally and some over many cities at once. Table 3-5 lists improvements and Wonders that can help fix your various resource dilemmas. Check the descriptions and tables in chapter VII for details on their effects.

TABLE 3-5. RESOURCE-BOOSTING IMPROVEMENTS AND WONDERS

RESOURCE	IMPROVEMENT	WONDER
Food	Granary, Harbor	Longevity, The Pyramids
Shields	Courthouse, Factory, Manufacturing Plant, Coal Plant, Hydro Plant, Nuclear Plant, Solar Plant, Offshore Platform	Forbidden Palace, Hoover Dam, Iron Works
Commerce	Airport, Bank, Harbor, Library, Marketplace, Research Lab, University	Copernicus's Observatory, Newton's University, SETI Program, Smith's Trading Company, The Colossus, Wall Street

NOTE

Most improvements and Wonders that affect commerce affect only one aspect—taxes, science, or luxuries. See the improvement and Wonder descriptions in chapter VII for details.

Better Governments Equal More Resources

The type of government you choose has a major impact on your cities' resource output. Primitive forms of government such as Despotism and Monarchy allow for less resource production than more advanced forms such as Republic and Democracy. Sometimes, a revolution is all you need to give your resource production a much-needed kick in the pants. (For details on governments and their effects, see chapter V.)

CITY MANAGEMENT

Now that you know how to read the terrain and select the perfect city site, you can just sit back and watch your cities thrive, right?

Wrong! Finding a good location and building the city are only the beginning. Despite the addition of smarter City Governors and the production queue, your cities cannot function at peak efficiency without your intervention—especially when they're just starting out. They need you to mold and shape them into valuable cogs in the well-oiled machine that is your empire.

This chapter examines the inner workings of cities, giving you hints and strategies to help you deal with the common problems encountered in city management.

YOUR CITIZENS

Without your citizens, your cities are nothing—literally! Cities in the *Civilization® III* game are defined by the number of citizens that dwell in them. The citizens do all the work that produces your resources and keeps your production going. So, it's not surprising that many of the top priorities of city management concern your population.

Population Growth

Your cities grow as a result of the amount of food they generate each turn. When the food storage box on the City Display fills up, the city gains another citizen.

The amount of food required for a city to grow is based on the city's size. *Civilization III* divides cities into three size classes:

- Town (population of 6 or less)
- City (population of 7–12)
- Metropolis (population of 13 or more)

The amount of food required for a city to grow is based on its class. The smaller the city class, the less food it needs to grow. So, Towns require a small accumulation of food for growth, Cities need more, and Metropolises need the most.

The higher your cities' populations, the more resources you gather. You want your cities to show steady growth. If a city is not producing a food surplus every turn, it cannot grow. If a city is producing less food that its citizens require, food is taken from the food storage box for that city every turn to cover the deficit. When the stored food is depleted, your population decreases by one. This cycle continues until the deficit is corrected.

TIP

A new trick that can help increase your food supply is clearing Forests. If you have Forest squares inside your city radius, have a Worker clear it. This turns the Forest into a square (usually Plains) that you can irrigate to produce more food for your city. And, in the process, 10 shields are added to the city's current production project!

Chapter III discusses some important strategies for increasing your food supply and city growth potential through terrain improvement and the construction of certain city improvements and Wonders of the World. If none of these tricks work, try switching to a more advanced form of government, where resource production is more fruitful. (See chapter V for details on the government types and their effects.)

TIP

Anarchy produces the least resources of any government type. When your empire falls into Anarchy (when you're switching governments, for instance) your cities probably can't produce enough food to support their populations. Make sure that all of your cities have an adequate food supply reserve before you switch governments.

If, after all of your efforts, you find that your city *still* has a growth problem, you chose a poor city site. Re-read chapter III for helpful tips in that area.

Dealing with Unhappiness

After you get your people producing the resources you need and growing your cities, the *real* problems begin. Everything is fine for a while, but eventually you begin to notice rumbles of discontent throughout

your empire. Your people are growing unhappy. What are you going to do about it?

The Causes of Unhappiness

At first, the most common cause of unhappiness is the size of your cities. A side effect of population growth is increasing unhappiness among your cities' populations. The first few citizens in every city are "born" content. After that, all of your citizens are automatically unhappy unless they're appeased. The higher the game's difficulty level, the more of an issue this becomes. (Table 2-3 in chapter II shows the exact numbers.)

> **NOTE**
>
> In the previous *Civilization* games, the number of cities you controlled could also cause unhappiness if your empire grew beyond a certain size. This is no longer the case in *Civilization III*.

Although this is most frequently the root of your troubles, other factors affect your peoples' happiness as well.

War Weariness

Another factor that causes unhappiness is war weariness. Under Republics and Democracies, war weariness arises when you are at war or are maintaining a warlike posture—stationing or operating units inside enemy territory—for an extended period of time. The effects of war weariness

are magnified if you are the one who declares war. (The effects are actually decreased significantly if your neighbor declares war on *you*.) The longer the war goes on, the more pronounced the unhappiness effects.

> **TIP**
>
> *War weariness is the new version of the Senate from the previous games—those pesky guys who always overruled your decision to declare war. You're no longer technically prevented from declaring war under Republics and Democracies, but the effects of war weariness are so great that you'd better make sure you can win the war quickly. Otherwise, you'll be forced to end the war due to rampant civil disorder.*

Resistance

Resistance goes hand in hand with war weariness. When you capture an opposing city in *Civilization III*, the population of the city retains its nationality. That means that, when you're playing the Romans and you capture an Egyptian city, the existing inhabitants are still Egyptians despite the fact that the city belongs to the Roman Empire.

Resistance takes place in captured cities when you remain at war with the civilization that previously controlled the city. Resisting citizens do not produce resources for the city, and you must compensate for this lack of productivity and their bad attitude until they come around. The following factors determine how quickly the resistance ends:

- **Your level of Culture:** The more Culture Points you have, the faster they'll calm down.
- **Availability of luxuries:** The more luxuries, the better, especially if your luxury rate is much higher than that of their former empire.
- **Your current form of government:** Advanced governments, with their higher levels of personal freedom, tend to quell the resistance faster.

Resistance takes place in your own cities as well. When an enemy captures one of your cities, the resistance movement in the city might even be strong enough to cause the city to revert back to your control without your having to recapture it.

NOTE

Resistance doesn't occur when you recapture a city that originally belonged to you. Because the citizens retain their nationality for some time after capture, citizens in liberated cities are still your people. Why would your own people resist?

TIP

Here's a useful (if ruthless) trick you can use to quell resistance in captured cities. If you're governing with Despotism or Communism, you can used forced labor—expending citizens to rush production—to thin out the indigenous population. Just keep rushing production projects until the city's population is down to one, and then let it start growing again. All of the new citizens "born" in the city are citizens of your empire, not that of the previous owner. (Under other governments, you can achieve the same effect by building multiple Settlers or Workers.)

Civil Disorder

A city experiences civil disorder.

Unhappiness comes to a head when the unhappy citizens outnumber the happy ones. At this point, the city enters a state of civil disorder. Avoid this situation

because a city in disorder cannot produce units, improvements, or Wonders. No taxes and sciences are generated as long as the disorder persists.

This has devastating and potentially far-reaching effects on your empire. The reduced tax revenues can tip your unit support and improvement maintenance budget into the red, and the lost science slows your research efforts.

Other effects of civil disorder include the possible collapse of your government into Anarchy (if you're in a Democracy and the state of civil disorder continues for multiple turns), and the possibility of Nuclear Plant meltdown in the affected cities.

When a city falls into this unfortunate state, it's not the end of the world—as long as you take care of the problem quickly. The following methods are all effective in eliminating civil disorder in the short-run:

- Rush-build a happiness-inducing improvement in the city.

- Turn one or more of the city's citizens into Entertainers.

- Increase the city's luxuries, either by raising your empire's luxury rate or connecting the city to luxury resources.

All of these unhappiness solutions are discussed in detail in the next section.

Preventing Unhappiness

There are many means at your disposal to rectify unhappiness when it becomes a problem. Better still, you can do lots of things prevent it before it *becomes* a problem.

Increasing Luxuries

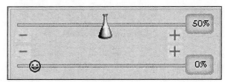

The luxury rate slider

Luxury items make people happy, and *Civ® III* offers two means through which you can increase the level of luxuries your citizens enjoy.

The first is a global luxury solution. Raise the percentage of commerce that is dedicated to luxuries by adjusting the sliders on the Domestic Advisor's screen. This affects all your cities simultaneously.

The global luxury solution is one of the most effective ways to prevent unhappiness, but it has a serious drawback. When you increase the luxury rate, you're drawing commerce away from either taxes or science (or both). If the tax rate's too low, you'll have trouble paying unit support and improvement upkeep. If the science rate's too low, your research efforts slow to a crawl and your opponents have a chance to get ahead of you technologically. If you need to raise the luxury rate so far that science and taxes suffer, seek other alternatives to your happiness problem.

Another option for raising luxury rates is to make sure your cities have access to as many luxury resources as possible. (Table 3-3 in chapter III lists all the available luxury resources.) If any luxury resources lie within any city radius, build a road to the resource and then build roads from that city to all of your other cities. Connected cities share luxury resources, each of which makes one content citizen happy or one unhappy citizen content. Monitor the effects of luxury resources by checking each city's luxury box on the City Display.

The City Display luxury box.

NOTE

Each "happy face" icon indicates one citizen that is being made happy by the item to which the happy face is attached. For example, each luxury resource in the luxury box in the figure above shows that one content citizen in the city is being made happy by each luxury resource.

Entertainers

One way to help eliminate unhappiness on a local level is to convert citizens to Entertainers. Entertainers are "specialists"— citizens who perform a specialized task rather than collecting resources for the city. (The two other specialists in the game are Scientists and Tax Collectors.) The game manual explains how to create an Entertainer when you need one. Every Entertainer makes one content citizen in the city happy.

Although there is technically no limit to the number of Entertainers a city can have, there is a *practical* limit. Every citizen you remove from the workforce to create a specialist decreases the city's resource output. If you create too many specialists, the city—and, eventually, your empire—will suffer.

View Entertainers as a short-term remedy for unhappiness. If you need more than one Entertainer in each city to maintain happiness for long periods of time, it's a pretty good indicator that something's wrong.

Martial Law

Under any system of government except Republic and Democracy, some of the military units you station in your cities contribute to happiness. Each eligible unit in your garrison makes one unhappy citizen content. (See the government descriptions in chapter V for details on how many units can be used to induce happiness under each system of government.)

This method is ideal for inducing happiness early in the game, and it becomes especially important when playing at the higher difficulty levels. But don't become too dependent on martial law as a source of happiness if you intend to switch to a Republic or a Democracy later. If your citizens are being kept at bay by your garrison, all unhappiness will break loose when you switch to a government that doesn't allow martial law. Transition to more permanent happiness maintenance methods before you move on to the more advanced governments.

Another drawback to this strategy is the support costs for the units. If you have a large empire, the price of supporting large numbers of garrisoned units becomes prohibitive.

Happiness-Inducing Improvements and Wonders

The best way to ensure long-term happiness in your cities is by building happiness-inducing city improvements and Wonders of the World. Their presence has a constant effect on your population, keeping unhappiness at bay in most situations. Table 4-1 lists all of the improvements and Wonders that affect happiness. Unless otherwise stated, the improvement or Wonder affects only the city in which it is built.

TABLE 4-1. IMPROVEMENTS AND WONDERS THAT AFFECT HAPPINESS

IMPROVEMENT/WONDER	EFFECT
IMPROVEMENTS	
Cathedral	Makes 3 unhappy citizens content
Colosseum	Makes 2 unhappy citizens content
Marketplace	Increases the number of "happy faces" produced by luxuries
Police Station	Reduces the effects of war weariness
Temple	Makes 1 unhappy citizen content
WONDERS	
Cure for Cancer	Makes 1 unhappy citizen content *in every city*
The Hanging Gardens	Makes 3 unhappy citizens content in its city, and 1 unhappy citizen content *in all of your other cities*
JS Bach's Cathedral	Makes 2 unhappy citizens content *in every city on the continent*
The Oracle	Doubles the effects of all Temples in your cities
Shakespeare's Theater	Makes all unhappy citizens in the city content
Sistine Chapel	Doubles the effects of all Cathedrals in your cities
Universal Suffrage	Reduces the effects of war weariness *in all of your cities*

Although their effects on happiness are indirect, improvements and Wonders that increase commerce also have an effect on happiness. More commerce means more luxuries.

TIP

You can instantly end civil disorder in a city by rush-building a happiness-inducing improvement or Wonder. This can be an expensive proposition, but it's a fast way to get your city back to normal and keep it that way for a while.

We Love the King Day

One way you know you're keeping your people happy is We Love the King Day (WLTKD). Cities celebrate WLTKD whenever more than half of the city's population is happy, and it continues for as long as that condition exists.

Cities celebrating WLTKD receive a healthy production bonus, significantly improving the state of your cities and your empire as a whole. Obviously, you want to foster this situation if at all possible. To do

so, keep your luxury rate as high as you can, make sure all your cities are connected so that they can share their luxury resources, and build as many happiness improvements and Wonders as you possibly can.

SHIELDS AND PRODUCTION

Your cities are your production centers. They construct the units, improvements, and Wonders that form the substance and military force of your civilization. At the heart of these production efforts is the city's shield output. Dealing with production is second only to population control when it comes to good city management.

Dealing with Shield Shortages

As with any other resource, shields are sometimes in short supply. Although shield deficits are no longer a unit-support problem in *Civilization III* (because unit support is now drawn from your treasury rather than your cities' shield output), lack of shields can still become a problem.

The best solution to shield shortage is prevention. Chapter III gives you some good tips on finding the right mix of terrain to maximize your cities' resource production. But, you can't always build your cities in shield-rich areas. Luckily, there are plenty of solutions to shield shortage problems.

Manually Adjust Your City Production

As described in chapter III, you can adjust a city's workforce to maximize the resources you need the most. Simply move your workers to terrain types that produce more shields—Hills and Mountains, for instance. Just don't overdo it. In your quest for shields, make sure that you don't create a food deficit!

Disband Old Units

As the game progresses, it's not uncommon to accumulate out-of-date military units. Maybe they were out in the field for a long time, or fortified and forgotten inside your cities. Either way, they pile up, and you might as well put them to good use if you don't need them anymore. Simply activate the unit, move it to the city that needs shields, and disband the unit. The resulting shields are added to the city's current production project. Disbanding units doesn't give you a huge number of shields—it won't even put a dent in the production of a Wonder, for instance—but it beats paying support for a unit you don't need anymore.

> **NOTE**
>
> In addition to being on the "gold standard," your units are now supported centrally—directly from your treasury. The concepts of unit "home cities" and the direct support of units by individual cities no longer exist in *Civilization III*.

Logging

Civilization III offers a new way to give a city's shield output a one-time boost. If you give the command, your Worker units can clear Forest squares for resources. You get 10 shields for each Forest cleared. The Forest doesn't have to be inside the city radius to provide this benefit. When an outlying Forest is cleared, the shields go to the nearest city.

While this is just the ticket to boosting the production of a crucial unit, improvement, or Wonder, remember that, once the Forest is cleared, you lose the resources it provided. (Forest squares generally revert to Plains when they're cleared.)

Shield-Enhancing Improvements and Wonders

A number of improvements and Wonders enhance your cities' shield output. Next to building the city in a shield-rich area, building these structures is the most effective and permanent way to keep your cities producing an adequate number of shields.

Table 4-2 lists all of the improvements and Wonders that enhance shield output. Unless otherwise noted, the improvement or Wonder affects only the city in which it's built.

TABLE 4-2. IMPROVEMENTS AND WONDERS THAT AFFECT SHIELD OUTPUT

IMPROVEMENT/WONDER	EFFECT
Coal Plant*	Increases Factory output by 50%
Courthouse	Reduces the amount of waste in the city.
Factory	Increases shield output by 50%
Hydro Plant*	Increases Factory output by 50%
Manufacturing Plant	Increases shield output by 50% (cumulative with Factory)
Nuclear Plant*	Increases Factory output by 50%
Offshore Platform	Causes all Coast, Sea, and Ocean squares in the city radius to produce one shield.
Solar Plant*	Increases Factory output by 50%
Forbidden Palace	Gives the benefits of a second palace in the city (zero waste).
Hoover Dam**	Acts as a Hydro Plant *in all of the cities on the continent where it is built*.
Iron Works	Increases shield output by 100% in the city where it's built (cumulative with existing improvements and Wonders).

* Only one type of power plant can exist in any one city.

** The effects of Hoover Dam are not cumulative with existing power plants.

Production Strategies

Starting on the turn you build your first city, you are producing. Units, improvements, Wonders—it never stops. Your cities all have "Governors" that control their various processes, including production. (See the sidebar, "Governing the City Governor," later in this chapter for details.) Even though you can let your cities run on automatic, it's best if you monitor their progress and lend a guiding hand— *especially* when it comes to production.

Here are a few general strategies to follow when it comes to your cities' production process:

- **Prioritize your production needs.** Choose production items based on the needs of your city. Make sure the city is protected and the citizens' needs are provided for before you start building extravagant Wonders.

- **Don't build beyond your means.** Remember, almost every improvement and unit sucks some Gold from your treasury each turn. Watch your balance sheet and don't build more than you can afford.

- *You* **pick the projects.** Your City Governors try to anticipate your needs, but they're often wrong. The only way to make sure your cities produce what you want them to produce is to make the choices yourself.

- **Read the production messages.** Every time a city produces something, a message appears telling you what was built *and* what Governor is planning to build next. Cities no longer build the same thing over and over until you tell them to stop—they pick new items on their own. Make sure you change production when the message appears if you don't want to build the item the City Governor has chosen.

- **Use the production queue.** Ensure that your city produces the items you want in the order you want them built by using the production queue. When you open the Production menu on the City Display, hold [Shift] and click the units/improvements/Wonders one at a time in the order you want them built. The city produces these items in the order you specified until it either completes the list or you change production manually. This greatly reduces the amount of micromanagement you have to perform.

- **Build your Wonders in shield-rich cities.** Because of their high cost, Wonders take forever to build in cities where shield output is low.

- **Think production changes through.** Before you decide to switch production in mid-stream, look at the relative costs of the two items. If the item in production is expensive and you've already spent a lot of shields on it, switching to a cheaper item wastes any extra shields beyond the second item's cost. Avoid this situation whenever possible.

- **Draft units in wartime:** You are allowed to draft a certain number of citizens into military service in each of your cities (the number varies by government type). This can save you time and shields when you're at war. Use this method sparingly,

though—it depletes your population, and the units it produces have fewer hit points (see Chapter VIII).

> **NOTE**
>
> The *Civilization II* penalty for switching production between units, improvements, and Wonders in mid-production no longer exists. You can now switch projects at will without suffering a penalty.

The High Cost of Rush Jobs

> **Domestic Advisor**
>
> Hurrying Horseman could cost the lives of 1 citizens.
>
> ◔ It's that important. Get out my whip!
> ◔ Oh, Really. Well never mind, then.
> ◎

"Rush jobs"—paying to complete the production of a unit, improvement, or Wonder—have always been quite expensive, but in *Civilization III*, the price of this action might be higher than you're willing to pay. The cost depends on your form of government.

Under Monarchy, Republic, and Democracy, you pay dearly in Gold for the completion of the project at hand—four Gold for every shield remaining in the project, to be precise. This is the rush job payment method that's familiar to veteran *Civ* players.

Under Despotism and Communism, the method of payment is different. Instead of paying Gold, you must *sacrifice members of the city's population* to rush the project. Obviously, this isn't something to undertake lightly.

No matter how you slice it, rush jobs exact a high price. Rather than paying that price, exercise other options before you empty your treasury or wipe out your population, such as:

- Clearing forests
- Disbanding old units
- Temporarily relocating your workers to shield-rich terrain

> **NOTE**
>
> You cannot rush the production of Wonders or Small Wonders. The only way to speed their production (other than the normal shield-optimizing tricks) is to use a Leader to finish them off. See chapter VIII for more info on Leaders.

GOVERNING THE CITY GOVERNOR

The City Governor window

Most of your time in the game is spent managing your cities. This is especially true later in the game, when you have dozens of cities to tend to every turn. It's easy to lose track of what's going on everywhere. That fact, more than anything else, leads to mistakes that cause civil unrest and other city management problems.

Civilization III addresses this problem by adding the City Governor—a series of detailed settings that you can set and forget that allow you to "program" your cities to run the way you want them to.

The City Governor contains two sets of controls. The General controls allows you to dictate, in broad strokes, the duties you want the game to attempt automatically—resource emphasis, whether or not to manage production projects, and so on. The Production controls allow you to set

the fine details of city production—whether to produce certain unit types, what types of improvements to build, and so on. The specifics of each setting are explained in the game manual.

When all of the City Governor General settings are turned off, you're on your own city management-wise, with the exception that your production queue tries to anticipate what unit or improvement you want to build next if you don't specify a project. This is a perfect for you veterans who like to control your own cities.

For those of you who like things a little more automatic, fiddle with the Governor settings and watch the results. With a little practice, you'll find the settings that best suit your style of play. Just remember— you *have* to specify exactly what you want if you want the City Governor to work for you. Here are a couple of general tips:

- **Be specific.** Leaving the Production settings on "Sometimes" across the board gives you the same random mix you get when the Governor is turned off.

- **Fine tune for best results.** Very seldom do you need all of your cities doing the same thing at the same time. When tweaking your Governor settings, set options by continent or individual city rather than using the "All Cities" setting.

Learning to squeeze the best results out of the City Governor takes a while but, when you do, the result is rewarding and relieves you of a lot of micromanagement duties.

TAXES AND FINANCE

While you're busy managing your population and production, it's easy to forget to monitor your treasury. At the start of the game, it usually grows steadily, but as the game progresses, improvement maintenance and unit support can cause it to dwindle. Money might not be your primary concern when it comes to city management, but you can't ignore it entirely.

Dealing with Financial Difficulties

You receive Gold from many different sources—gifts from other civilizations during negotiations, booty from villages ("goodie huts"), and bounty for destroying Barbarian strongholds are just a few of the many ways to make money. Your primary funds, however, come from your cities' commerce in the form of taxes.

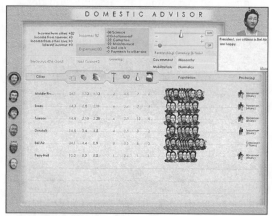

The Domestic Advisor's screen

From the time you build your first city, you can monitor your financial situation from the Domestic Advisor's screen. The upper-left corner shows your current balance sheet and lets you see whether you're making money, losing money, or just breaking even. (In fact, this screen provides you with an at-a-glance report on all of the resource production in each of your cities—it's a valuable city and empire managing resource!)

When your Gold income doesn't cover your expenses, your treasury begins to shrink. When you start receiving warnings to this effect, take heed! When your treasury runs out, some of your improvements might be sold or your units disbanded to compensate for the deficit.

> **NOTE**
>
> On the Chieftain and Warlord difficulty levels, the game doesn't automatically sell off your improvements or disband your units when the treasury hits zero.

Monitor your financial situation frequently throughout the game. As with any resource deficit, prevention is always preferable to compensation. However, if you *do* run into financial difficulties, you have a number of ways to bolster your sagging treasury.

Increasing the Tax Rate

One solution is to increase the amount of incoming commerce that is dedicated to tax revenue. Do this by adjusting the science and luxury sliders on the Domestic Advisor's screen. The percentage of each of these commerce components shows on their respective sliders. Add the two together and subtract the number from 100, and that's your tax percentage. The higher the percentage, the more Gold you collect each turn. Watch the tax income increase and decrease on the balance sheet as you move the sliders.

Increasing the tax rate has drawbacks. First, increasing taxes decreases the amount of commerce dedicated to science and luxuries.

Increasing the tax rate beyond a certain level also causes unhappiness among your population. (Watch the faces on the Domestic Advisor's screen as you move the sliders—they react dynamically.) In fact, if you bump the rate too high, you'll send cities into civil disorder, which actually *decreases* your tax income.

Use this method of increasing your income used as a stopgap measure until a more permanent solution can be found. Commerce is almost always better spent on science and luxuries.

Tax Collectors

Tax Collectors, like Entertainers, are specialists—citizens pulled from the workforce to serve the greater good of the city. Every Tax Collector you add to a city increases the city's tax income by a small amount.

Like raising taxes, creating Tax Collectors should only be used as a temporary solution to your money problems. Every Tax Collector robs your city of resources that the citizens would otherwise harvest. This can cause shortages of shields and food, replacing one resource problem with another.

Disbanding Units

Now that unit support is drawn from your treasury, just about every unit you build costs you money every turn. One common source of cash problems is the accumulation of outdated units that have been forgotten in some obscure corner of the map.

When your finances dip into the red, search all of your cities and the terrain throughout your territory for units you're not using anymore. Move these extraneous units to your cities and disband them as soon as you can. Not only will you decrease your expenses, you'll also add some shields to the production projects in the cities where you disband the units.

Selling Improvements

When times are really tough, you can sell your city improvements for some quick cash. You can only sell one improvement each turn.

This is obviously a last-resort method of raising Gold. If you get into a situation where this is your only course of action, you're doing something wrong. If you must sell improvements, chose them based first on their importance (the less it will impact the city, the better) and second on the maintenance cost (selling improvements with high maintenance costs has a greater impact on your per-turn outlay of Gold).

> **TIP**
>
> Never *sell an improvement that is generating tax revenue or commerce to make ends meet. That's just plain counterproductive.*

Wealth

Right from the beginning of the game, there is an item called "Wealth" listed at the bottom of every city's production menu. This useful little item is unlike any other production item. Instead of producing a unit, improvement, or Wonder, cities producing Wealth convert all of their shield output into cold, hard cash that is added to your treasury at the beginning of each turn.

When you need Gold—or, when there's simply nothing else you need to build at the moment—have one or more of your cities produce Wealth. This is a convenient way to add to your treasury with very little fuss.

> **TIP**
>
> *If you use Wealth frequently for extra cash, research Economics as soon as you can. The conversion rate of shields to Gold is twice as high after you discover Economics.*

Interest Income

There's nothing like putting your cash reserves to work for you, and in *Civilization III* there's a Small Wonder that lets you do just that.

If you build Wall Street in one of your cities, the money in your treasury earns interest every turn. It's as simple as that. The higher your balance, the higher your interest income (up to a maximum of 50 Gold per turn). No matter what your financial state, do yourself a favor and take the free money!

Switch Governments

Sometimes, all you need to do to improve your finances is switch to a better form of government. The more advanced your government, the higher your commerce output. Better governments—especially Republics and Democracies—also exhibit lower corruption. Because corruption robs you of valuable commerce, your tax income potential rises as corruption declines.

Moneymaking Improvements and Wonders

As is the case with most resource problems, one of the best ways to prevent money troubles is to equip your cities with improvements and Wonders that increase tax revenue or commerce output in general. Table 4-3 lists the improvements and Wonders that do just that. Unless otherwise noted, the improvements and Wonders listed affect only the city in which they're built.

TABLE 4-3. MONEYMAKING IMPROVEMENTS AND WONDERS

IMPROVEMENT/WONDER	EFFECT
Bank	Increases tax revenue by 50% (cumulative with Marketplace).
Courthouse	Reduces corruption
Marketplace	Increases tax revenue by 50%
Wealth	Converts shields output to Gold.
Forbidden Palace	Provides the benefits of a Palace (eliminates corruption in the city where it's built).
Smith's Trading Company	Pays maintenance costs of all commerce-related improvements *in every city*.
Wall Street	Treasury earns 5% interest per turn (50 Gold per turn maximum).

POLLUTION

A negative byproduct of a growing civilization is pollution. In most cases, you don't have to worry about pollution until about the middle of the game, shortly after you and your opponents enter the Industrial Age. From that point on, the threat of pollution is an ever-present demon that you have to deal with.

What Causes Pollution?

The primary contributors to pollution are city population and the combined Pollution Points of the city improvements and Wonders in *all of your cities combined*. The equation used to determine whether pollution appears inside a city's radius each turn is as follows: *(Total Pollution Points)+ (1 per citizen over 12) = Percent chance of pollution per turn.*

This equation is run for each of your cities at the start of every turn.

Pollution Points replace the city's shield output as the primary pollution factor in *Civilization III*. (That's right—the number of shields a city produces has *no* bearing on its pollution output.) The pollution-producing improvements and Wonders and the number of Pollution Points they generate each turn are listed in table 4-4.

TABLE 4-4.
IMPROVEMENTS AND WONDERS THAT POLLUTE

IMPROVEMENT/WONDER	POLLUTION POINTS
Airport	1
Coal Plant	2
Factory	2
Iron Works	4
Manufacturing Plant	2
Offshore Platform	2
Research Lab	1

You can monitor each city's pollution potential at a glance by looking at the pollution box on the City Display.

Pollution Effects

You are notified every time a terrain square in your empire becomes polluted, and the affected terrain is marked with a pollution icon.

Pollution sullies the land.

Pollution robs your land of vital resources. In fact, it reduces all resource production on the affected square by 50 percent! For example, a terrain square that normally produces one food, two shields, and two commerce, produces one food, one shield, and one commerce when polluted.

Pollution Solutions

Get rid of pollution as soon as possible when it starts to appear. The effects it has on your resource output is bad enough when only one terrain square is polluted. If more pollution appears, things get progressively worse.

You can do several things to deal with pollution when it appears and to prevent it from appearing in the first place.

Assign Workers to Clean Up Detail

One of the functions your Workers can perform is cleaning polluted terrain. Simply move a Worker to the polluted terrain square and click the Clean Pollution icon. In the Industrial Age, when pollution often runs rampant and there are no easy ways to stop it, assign a couple of Workers in each geographic area of your empire to perform cleanup tasks on a full-time basis. If you automate the Worker using Shift+P the unit will clean up all of the pollution in the area while ignoring all other Worker tasks.

Eco-Friendly Improvements

A number of improvements and Wonders help reduce pollution output so there's less chance of pollution occurring. The Hydro, Nuclear, and Solar Plants are pollution-free alternatives to the Coal Plant for increasing shield output in a city. Avoid Coal Plants whenever possible. Table 4-5 lists several other improvements that have a positive effect in your fight against pollution.

TABLE 4-5.
POLLUTION-REDUCING IMPROVEMENTS

IMPROVEMENT	EFFECT
Mass Transit System	Reduces the pollution caused by population
Recycling Center	Reduces the pollution caused by improvements and Wonders

Unfortunately, neither of these are available until Modern Times. That means that earlier in the game you must avoid building too many improvements that pollute, mobilize your Workers to remove pollution when it occurs, and be ready to build Mass Transit and Recycling Centers in all of your cities as soon as they become available.

Global Warming

 Just as polluted terrain is a result of your empire's pollution output, global warming is a result of *worldwide* pollution output. When the amount of pollution produced by all civilizations combined reaches critical levels, catastrophic environmental effects result.

> **NOTE**
>
> Global warming has also changed in *Civilization III*. If you're used to the old system from the previous games, read on to discover what's new.

Global warming is no longer tied to the number of polluted terrain squares that exist in the world. *Civilization III* determines whether global warming occurs by taking into account the total population of all cities in the world and the total number of Pollution Points produced by the improvements and Wonders in every city.

The higher these numbers become, the higher the chance of a global warming event.

As you might expect, when global warming occurs, the temperature rises all over the planet. This transforms terrain in coastal areas into wetter terrain—Plains and Grasslands transform into Flood Plains and Jungles, for instance. Farther inland, the opposite occurs. Grasslands and Plains are transformed into arid Desert Squares in many locations.

Obviously, you want to avoid global warming if at all possible. Unfortunately, you have no control whatsoever over your opponents' pollution. However, you can do your part to help stop global warming by making sure your cities are as pollution-free as possible. (See "Pollution Solutions" earlier in this chapter for some helpful tips.)

> **TIP**
>
> *The chance of global warming increases every time a nuclear explosion occurs. Each successive atomic blast exponentially increases the chance for global warming. One of the best ways to prevent global warming is to avoid nuclear warfare at all costs.*

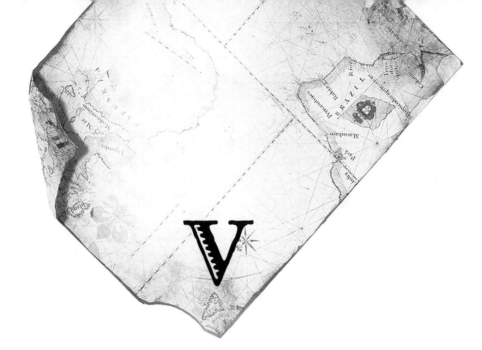

EMPIRE MANAGEMENT

Although good city management skills are vital to your success in the *Civilization® III* game, there's a broader view to consider. Your cities are but individual cogs in the vast machine that is your empire. While you're squaring away your city-related issues, always keep the welfare of your entire empire in mind.

This chapter takes a look at the elements that affect the macro-management of your civilization beyond the city level and your interaction with opponents. Here, you'll gain valuable insight into choosing the right government, dealing with the new Culture element of the game, the finer points of trade and diplomacy, and the backstabbing world of espionage.

SYSTEMS OF GOVERNMENT

Five systems of government are available in *Civ® III* (six, if you count Anarchy). Whether you like it or not, you start out governing through Despotism. The other government types become available over time through research. Each government type favors a different gameplay style, and you need to know the benefits and drawbacks of each before you can decide which is right for you.

The following sections describe the pros and cons of each government type in detail. Table 5-1 shows the government effects and statistics at a glance. The effects and statistics listed are as follows:

- **Resource Output:** The effects of the government on the output of food, shields, and commerce.

- **Corruption/Waste:** The level of corruption and waste (shields and taxes lost to graft and inefficiency).

- **Free Units:** The number of units per Town/City/Metropolis that do not require you to pay the normal one Gold per turn support cost.

- **Martial Law Units:** The number of units per city that can be placed in the city's garrison that have a positive effect on the happiness of the city's population. (Each unit makes one unhappy citizen content.)

- **Rush Job Method:** The cost of rushing production jobs (completing units or improvements by paying for them).

- **Additional Features:** Other miscellaneous effects of the government type.

TABLE 5-1. GOVERNMENT EFFECTS AND STATISTICS

GOVERNMENT	RESOURCE OUTPUT	CORRUPTION/WASTE	MARTIAL LAW UNITS	RUSH JOB METHOD	ADDITIONAL FEATURES
Anarchy	Food only (-1 food per square)	Catastrophic	0	None	Worker speed -50%; cannot produce units/improvements/Wonders; no research; cannot use propaganda
Despotism	Max. 2 food/shields/commerce per square	Rampant	2	Population loss	Can draft 2 citizens per city
Monarchy	Normal	Problematic	3	Pay Gold	Can draft 2 citizens per city
Republic	+1 commerce*	Nuisance	0	Pay Gold	Can draft 1 citizen per city; war weariness (low)
Communism	Normal	Communal	4	Population loss	Can draft 3 citizens per city; espionage missions have a higher chance of success
Democracy	+1 commerce*	Minimal	0	Pay Gold	Can draft 1 citizen per city; cities immune from propaganda; worker speed +50%; war weariness (high)

In terrain squares already producing commerce.

Anarchy

Technically, Anarchy isn't a form of government— it's actually a *lack* of centralized government. When you declare a revolution to change governments, your society temporarily enters a state of Anarchy until the new government can be established. You also experience Anarchy when your government falls as a result of extended periods of civil disorder.

Anarchy lasts only a few turns or so, but the results are always unpleasant. The huge drop in resource output, science, and production brings your empire to a grinding halt. So, before you launch a revolution, make sure there's a good reason to do so. And, to prevent an inadvertent slip into Anarchy, quell civil disorder as soon as possible when it occurs.

Despotism

At the start of the game, Despotism is the only type of government available. Of all the governments you can actively choose, it is by far the worst. Despotism allows you to expand your civilization and build up your military without penalty, but the resource output penalties and the level of corruption and waste are excellent

motivators to make your Despotic reign a short one. Make it a point to strive for either Monarchy or The Republic as early in the game as possible. (See chapter VI for some helpful research tips.)

Monarchy

Monarchy is one of the two government advances available in Ancient Times. This system of government offers many advantages over Despotism, especially if you decide to follow a military strategy. Commerce is lower than in a Republic, and corruption and waste are considerably higher. However, the greater number of free units, the ability to use martial law to make your citizens happy, and freedom from the shackles of war weariness make Monarchy your only logical choice if you choose to follow a conquest-oriented strategy—at least until Communism comes along.

What's the price of all this military freedom? Resources. Under a Monarchy, you enjoy no resource output bonus, and the shields and commerce you *do* produce are severely taxed by the high levels of corruption and waste. The commerce loss is offset somewhat by the large number of support-free units, but the corruption and waste problem becomes increasingly severe as your empire grows.

Republic

Republic is your second advanced government alternative in Ancient Times. Just as Monarchy favors the conquest-minded, Republic offers incentives to those who prefer to win through peaceful coexistence.

The up side of a Republic is enhanced resource output and usage. Your commerce output is significantly increased, which lets you spend more on luxuries and science (not to mention taxes) than you would have under a Monarchy. The significantly lower rate of waste and corruption further increases your level of commerce and boosts your effective shield output as well.

The cost of these benefits is lack of military freedom and the increased possibility of population unhappiness. You can't use martial law to make citizens happy, which forces you to compensate through improvements and Wonders. You must also pay support on every unit you have in service, which limits the number of units you can effectively field at any given time. The topper is war weariness, which prevents you from engaging in warlike activities for extended periods of time. For these reasons, Republics are most effective when you're playing a peaceful game.

Communism

Communism is the advanced government that offers the most benefits to those of you who enjoy the conquest game. While it lacks the resource bonuses of Republics and Democracies, it allows for the highest possible level of military activity.

The level of free unit support under Communism is identical to that of Monarchy. The martial law benefit is increased over Monarchy, as is the draft rate. Corruption and waste, while still greater than they are under a Democracy, are "communal." That is, all cities outside the capital suffer the same rate of corruption and waste—a considerably lower overall rate than that of a Monarchy. The best feature of Communism (from a military standpoint) is that there's no war weariness—a very helpful feature indeed when you're trying to take over the world by force.

Besides the lack of resource bonuses there is one additional downside to Communism: rush jobs. As with Despotism, the only way to rush the completion of a unit or an improvement under Communism is forced labor—that is, you sacrifice citizens to rush the production job. It's a small price to pay, perhaps, for being able to wage war with reckless abandon.

TIP

Never adopt a conquest strategy under any governments except Monarchy and Communism. However, if you're up for the challenge of waging war in a Democracy or a Republic, have plenty of Gold available to buy Culture and happiness-generating improvements in the cities you capture. Otherwise, assimilating them into your empire is nearly impossible under the "peacetime" governments.

Democracy

Like the Republic before it, Democracy is best suited for nonconquest strategies. It's the game's most advanced system of government— but it also demands your constant attention to detail, especially when it comes to population happiness.

Of all the government types available, Democracy has the lowest rate of corruption and waste. As in a Republic, you receive a commerce bonus. Because they are so happy and carefree, your Workers work at 150 percent of their speed under lower forms of government.

As always, there's a tradeoff for all of these benefits. In this case, it's war weariness. The effects of prolonged warfare under a Democracy cause unhappiness much faster than they do under a Republic.

That means that you must either stock up on happiness-inducing and war weariness–suppressing improvements and Wonders, or refrain from engaging in warlike activities.

TIP

If you're constantly increasing the number of Entertainers in your cities to quell unhappiness, switch to a less demanding system of government. Don't be ashamed, though—running a Democracy effectively is one of the most difficult tasks in the game, especially on high difficulty levels.

CORRUPTION AND WASTE

Corruption and waste exist to varying degrees under every form of government. Corruption is the loss of commerce due to dishonest practices (embezzlement, theft, and so on). Waste is the inefficient use of shields.

Your capital city doesn't experience corruption and waste, but most of your other cities do. The amount of corruption and waste a city suffers is based on the following factors:

- **Government type:** Each system of government experiences a different level of corruption and waste.

- **The city's distance from your capital:** The farther away from your capital, the higher the city's corruption and waste.

- **The number of cities in your empire:** The level of corruption and waste in your cities goes up incrementally. The more cities you have, the worse it gets.

The best overall method to counteract the effects of corruption and waste is to change to a form of government where corruption and waste are low. The corruption and waste levels from lowest to highest are:

1. Democracy

2. Republic

3. Communism

4. Monarchy

5. Despotism

Other methods of corruption and waste reduction include:

- **Courthouses:** Cities with Courthouses experience 50 percent less corruption and waste.

- **Forbidden Palace:** This Small Wonder acts as a second Palace, eliminating corruption and waste in the city where it's built.

- **Civilizations with Commercial tendencies:** When you play as a civilization with the civ-specific Commercial characteristic, you experience less corruption and waste. (See table 2-1 in chapter II.)

- **We Love the King Day:** When a city is celebrating this event, the level of waste (but not corruption) is slightly lower.

CULTURE

Culture is a new concept that has been introduced in *Civilization III*. This very subtle factor affects a wide variety of game elements from your empire's territorial boundaries to your opponents' perception of you during negotiations.

Accumulating Culture Points

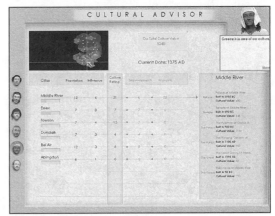

The Cultural Advisor's screen

Every turn, your civilization accumulates Culture Points. These points are added to a running total kept throughout the game. The number of points you generate each turn and your total number of accumulated points are displayed in the top right portion of the City Display. You can also monitor your empire's Culture by checking in with the Cultural Advisor.

Certain improvements and all Wonders of the World and Small Wonders generate Culture Points. The more of these Culture-generating structures you build in your empire, the more Culture Points you accumulate each turn. Check the Improvement Roster to see how many Culture Points are being generated by each improvement or Wonder in your city. The number of music note icons next to each Culture-generating structure shows how many points that structure generates each turn.

Table 5-2 lists the improvements that generate Culture Points. Table 5-3 lists the number of Culture Points generated by each Wonder and Small Wonder.

TABLE 5-2.
CULTURE-GENERATING IMPROVEMENTS

IMPROVEMENT	CULTURE POINTS PER TURN
Cathedral	3
Colosseum	2
Library	3
Palace	1
Research Lab	2
Temple	2
University	4

TABLE 5-3.
CULTURE POINTS GENERATED BY WONDERS

WONDER	CULTURE POINTS PER TURN
Apollo Program	3
Battlefield Medicine	1
The Colossus	3
Copernicus's Observatory	4
Cure for Cancer	5
Forbidden Palace	3
The Great Library	5
The Great Lighthouse	2
The Great Wall	2
The Hanging Gardens	4
Heroic Epic	4
Hoover Dam	3
Intelligence Agency	1
Iron Works	2
JS Bach's Cathedral	5
Leonardo's Workshop	2
Longevity	3
Magellan's Voyage	3
The Manhattan Project	2
Military Academy	1
Newton's University	5
The Oracle	4
The Pentagon	1
The Pyramids	4

continued on next page

TABLE 5-3, CONTINUED
CULTURE POINTS GENERATED BY WONDERS

WONDER	CULTURE POINTS PER TURN
SETI Program	3
Shakespeare's Theater	5
Sistine Chapel	4
Smith's Trading Company	3
Strategic Missile Defense	1
Sun Tzu's Art of War	2
Theory of Evolution	3
The United Nations	4
Universal Suffrage	4
Wall Street	2

The Effects of Culture

Culture affects your civilization in many ways. Each Cultural effect plays an important role in the expansion and/or prosperity of your empire.

Border Expansion

The most obvious effect of Culture is the progressive expansion of your empire's borders. Border expansion is triggered by the Culture Points accumulated by individual cities. Each time a city hits a certain Culture Point threshold, the city's border expands. As the game progresses,

your cities' cultural borders merge to form large contiguous areas of territory that you command.

Culture expands the empire's borders.

TIP

Your borders cannot expand beyond the borders of another civilization and vice-versa. To prevent an opponent's borders from expanding, build a couple of cities close to the opposing city and start building up your Culture. Eventually, you box in your opponent and keep his or her territorial expansion to a minimum. As a bonus, you might eventually assimilate the rival city. Once your cities' Culture levels are high enough, the rival city will eventually defect to your empire.

Border expansion is vital when you're attempting a Domination victory. To win in this manner, your borders must encompass two thirds of the planet's surface (see chapter IX). There are also a number of other advantages to territorial control:

- Your rivals cannot move along your roads or railroads in peacetime unless they first negotiate a right of passage agreement, and you can always eject enemy units from your territory during diplomatic negotiations.

- The terrain within your borders is visible at all times.

- Strategic and luxury resources within your borders can be gathered without building a colony.

TIP

Because your opponents cannot use roads in your territory without your permission, a great way to keep them from moving through your territory is to build roads in all of the terrain squares along common borders.

City Assimilation

When you capture a rival city, its inhabitants initially resist your rule. Resisting citizens do not produce resources, and they must be kept at bay by your military units (see chapter VIII).

The amount of time that it takes to assimilate a city into your empire depends on several factors, one of which is the number of Culture Points you have as compared to the city's previous owner. The more Culture you have, the shorter the period of resistance. The bigger the Cultural difference, the longer the assimilation period.

If your Culture is significantly better than that of your nearby rivals, their cities begin defecting to your empire of their own free will. This handy Culture effect often allows you to win through Domination without firing a single shot. To snare rival cities, simply build up the Culture in the cities closest to the rival's border. Eventually, they'll be begging to be a part of your Culturally-superior empire.

City Liberation

Another handy side effect of Culture helps you keep your empire intact when you're under fire. When your Culture is significantly higher than your enemy's, your captured cities have a good chance of liberating themselves and rejoining your empire without your having to fight for them. This is the same principle as assimilating rival cities through Culture, but your chances here are higher because the citizens in the city are yours. This facet of Culture alone should be enough to convince you to maintain a high Culture Point level even if your ultimate goal is conquest.

Negotiating Power

The Greek people are in awe of our culture.

More

Your opponents' Cultural perception of you is based on the relative differences between your Culture Point total and theirs. The higher your Culture is compared to an opponent's, the more respect the opponent has for you. Table 5-4 shows the perception ratings and the Culture Point ratio required to achieve each.

TABLE 5-4. DETERMINING THE CULTURAL PERCEPTION OF YOUR EMPIRE

CULTURE POINT RATIO (YOURS:THEIRS)	YOUR OPPONENT IS:
3:1	In awe of your empire
2:1	An admirer of your empire
1:1	Impressed with your empire
3:4	Unimpressed with your empire
1:2	Dismissive of your empire
1:3	Disdainful of your empire

> **NOTE**
> Although you never see it onscreen, your Cultural Opinion of your opponents follows the same set of rules as far as the game is concerned (your *personal* opinion of your opponents notwithstanding) for the purpose of determining the results of certain diplomatic and espionage actions.

Your opponents' perception of you figures heavily in the way opposing leaders act and react during diplomatic negotiations. When you have a large number of Culture Points compared to the empire you're negotiating with, their leader is more likely to react favorably to your proposals. Positive relationships, including trade agreements, peace treaties, and other pacts, are much easier to maintain when you Culturally outrank your opponent.

Propaganda

The higher your Culture, the less you fear propaganda—and the more it can work in your favor! A city's reaction to propaganda is based on the relative difference between the city's Culture Points and those of the empire launching the propaganda campaign, as well as government-based modifiers. The empire with the higher point value has a greater chance of launching a successful propaganda campaign, and a better chance resisting the propaganda of a Culturally-inferior empire.

For more details on propaganda, see the "Espionage" section later in this chapter.

TRADE

The Trade Advisor's screen

Trade has always been an important concept in *Civilization* but, in *Civilization III* it is even more so. There are two types of trade—domestic trade and foreign trade. Each plays an important role in empire management. Keep track of your domestic and foreign trade by checking the Trade Advisor's screen.

NOTE
The trade system has been completely revamped in *Civ III*. Veterans of the previous *Civilization* games should study this section for info on how the new system functions.

Domestic Trade

As the name implies, domestic trade takes place between the cities within your empire. This trade consists of the sharing of strategic and luxury special resources (see chapter III for a list of these resources). Strategic resources are required for the production of some units, and each luxury resource makes one unhappy citizen in each city with access to the resource content.

TIP
To take advantage of a luxury or strategic resource, simply build a road between it and one (or more) of your cities. Your citizens don't have to work the terrain to get the resource. In fact, the resource doesn't even need to be within the city radius of any of your cities—it only needs to be within your territory. You also can take advantage of luxury and strategic resources outside your territory by having a Worker construct a colony on the resource square.

To trade with one another, your cities must be connected. For cities on the same land mass, this is as simple as building roads or railroads to connect the cities. All cities connected in this manner share strategic and luxury resources available to any of the connected cities.

Roads obviously cannot connect cities on different continents. These cities must be connected in a different manner. Coastal cities can trade with other coastal cities if both cities have the Harbor improvement. Distant cities can also trade with one another over vast distances if both are equipped with Airports. Cities connected via Harbors or Airports share resources with all cities in the trade network just as if they were connected by roads.

A FEW FACTS ABOUT HARBORS

Harbors are tricky. For two cities to be connected, both must have Harbors with an unobstructed path of water squares between them (unexplored water terrain doesn't work).

But wait, there's more! Prior to the discovery of Astronomy, the trade route must stretch exclusively through Coast squares. Astronomy allows trade to take place across Sea squares as well, but not across Ocean squares. (That's not allowed until after you discover Magnetism or Navigation.)

Because an unobstructed route is required, a naval blockade can prevent a Harbor city from conducting trade. If opposing naval vessels block all of the possible outbound water routes from the city, overseas trade to that city is cut off.

Because of the importance of strategic and luxury resources, it is *absolutely imperative* to connect all of your cities to your trade network. (You can see which cities aren't connected to your trade network by checking the Unconnected Cities list on the Trade Advisor's screen.) Cities that aren't connected cannot share in the happiness effects of your luxury resources and can't produce valuable units on which their survival might depend.

NOTE

Trade—domestic or foreign—cannot take place across enemy territory. If you are at war with a civilization whose empire cuts across the roads that connect your cities, the road doesn't serve as a trade connection. The only way to keep these cut-off cities in your trade network is through the use of Harbors or Airports.

Foreign Trade

As long as all of your cities are connected to your trade network, a single luxury or strategic resource square is enough to supply the needs of your entire civilization. In other words, all of your cities benefit from the happiness generated by a single Silk square, and all can build mounted units if a single Horses square is accessible. Any additional luxury or strategic resource squares are considered surplus, and can be traded with other civilizations during negotiations. To trade resources with your neighbors, your empire must be connected to theirs, just as your own cities must be connected to share resources.

Luxury resources are some of your best bargaining chips in foreign trade. By trading luxuries with your opponents, you make them happy, and the luxuries you receive in return make your people happy. Whenever your opponents have luxuries to trade with you, take them up on their offer (or ask for the resources if they're not offering them on their own).

TIP

Whoever controls the luxury resources controls the game. Always take advantage of as many luxury resources as possible and guard them zealously.

Strategic resources are a little trickier. You can offer them to your neighbors in negotiations just as you can luxuries—but be careful about it. Remember, strategic resources allow you to produce military units. If your rival has no access to a particular strategic resource, that means he or she cannot produce units that require that resource. That could potentially give you a strong military advantage, depending on the resource. As a general rule, never trade a strategic resource to your neighbors unless you are sure you can defeat any units that that neighbor might build using

that resource. Having a military advantage over a neighbor is usually preferable to appeasing them in trade negotiations.

TIP

When you are at war with a rival civilization, all trade with that empire is cut off until hostilities cease. Make an effort to maintain good relations with your opponents with whom you have a good trade relationship. This is especially true if you're depending on traded luxury resources to keep your population happy.

DIPLOMACY

The Diplomacy interface

Diplomacy in *Civilization III* has been greatly expanded, and it plays an important role in your success. When you establish communications with a civilization (usually

by encountering one of their units in the field), you can engage in rudimentary discussions and trades of Gold and technology. But that's just the tip of the iceberg.

After you discover Writing, you can set up embassies in your opponents' capital cities (double-click the Capital City icon next to your opponent's capital to do so). At that point, you can enter into treaty negotiations and military alliances. Once you discover Map Making, you can trade world maps. Finally, after you research Nationalism, you can engage in mutual protection pacts and trade embargoes against other civilizations. On top of all of this, you can also trade strategic and luxury resources and even entire *cities* during diplomatic negotiations.

Obviously, the implications of all of these diplomacy options are huge, and many strategies can assist you in the diplomatic process.

Manipulating Diplomatic Attitude

What you need to offer your rivals to successfully complete a diplomatic transaction depends on their attitude toward you at the time. This is clear both from their facial expressions and the actual description of their attitude in the text box, which can be (from best to worst):

- Gracious
- Polite
- Cautious
- Annoyed
- Furious

Controlling your opponents' diplomatic demeanor is a difficult balancing act. Many factors combine to determine your opponents' opinions of your civilization. The most important include:

- **Prior positive negotiations.** The more times you have dealt fairly with a civilization, the happier they are to see you in successive negotiations.

- **Honoring treaties.** The more treaties you violate with the civilization in question, the lower their opinion of you. Violating treaties with others also figures into this equation.

- **War.** Civilizations you've been at war with are less likely to hold you in high esteem.

- **Culture.** The higher your opponent's Cultural perception of your empire, the better you'll be treated. (See table 5-4.)

- **Military strength.** When your military units outnumber your opponent's, you are treated with more respect.

- **Scientific achievements.** Your rivals tend to be nicer to you if you are significantly ahead of them advance-wise.

NOTE

Your opponents' actions, as well as their negotiations with you, reflect their attitude toward you. For example, if you habitually break treaties with others, your opponents are more likely to do the same to you. The Golden Rule of Diplomacy is: Do unto other civilizations as you would have them do unto your own.

Global Cultures

This concept is not related to Culture Points, but it affects negotiations in a similar way in some cases.

The game's civilizations are divided into five global cultures. Each global culture shares the same city style and their citizens look the same. Generally, civilizations within a given global culture start in the same general area of the map.

Civilizations that share the same global culture as the tribe you're playing tend to be more tolerant of you during negotiations. Table 5-5 breaks down the civilizations by global culture.

TABLE 5-5.
CIVILIZATIONS BY GLOBAL CULTURE

GLOBAL CULTURE	MEMBER CIVILIZATIONS
American	Americans, Aztecs, Iroquois
Asian	Chinese, Indian, Japanese
European	English, French, Germans, Russians
Mediterranean	Egyptians, Greeks, Romans
Mid East	Babylonians, Persians, Zulus

The Foreign Advisor

I doubt they will accept this proposal.

More

One of the most helpful diplomatic tools at your disposal is the Foreign Advisor. All of your advisors give you helpful pointers when you consult them, but none compare to the Foreign Advisor's wisdom.

When you're working out a diplomatic deal, watch the Advisor's advice window. As you add items to the negotiation "table," the Advisor gives you a very accurate opinion of what your rival thinks of the deal as it currently stands. If you follow his advice, your negotiations are bound to go well. When he tells you that your opponent will "probably find this proposal acceptable," he or she probably will. When he tells you that your opponent will "be insulted by this proposal," watch out for the diplomatic consequences if you propose the deal in spite of the Advisor's warning! By heeding the Foreign Advisor's advice, you can be assured of a viable deal every time.

In addition to his wise deal-making advice, the Foreign Advisor gives you lots of incidental information about your opponent. You can find out your opponent's Cultural perception of your empire (see table 5-4), their military strengths and weaknesses, and their relative level of technology. All of this information helps you prepare for future diplomatic (and military) encounters.

Map Trading Advice

As mentioned earlier, after you research Map Making, you can trade maps with your opponents during diplomatic exchanges. You can trade two types of maps—world maps (which show the position and particulars of everything you've explored), or territory maps (which show only Cultural borders and city positions). Of the two,

world maps are the most valuable because they reveal a great deal more information.

Use map trading to explore the world without sending units out. By simply trading maps with civilizations you meet, you greatly expand your knowledge of world geography and the size of neighboring empires. Further exploit map trading by negotiating with your neighbors for contact with other civilizations that they have encountered but you haven't met yet. Once you're in contact with them, you can trade maps with them as well.

TIP

The relative value of your world map in diplomatic negotiations changes over time. It is never more valuable to your opponents as it is when you first meet. Exploit this by offering to sell them your world map for a high price. (Watch the Foreign Advisor to make sure you're not asking for too much.) Further increase your map profits by negotiating for communications with civilizations that you haven't met yet and then selling them your map.

Technology Trading Advice

One of the most common requests your opponents make in diplomatic negotiations is for a trade of civilization advances. It's always helpful when *you* receive advances, but be careful of what advances you trade away to *them*.

As a general rule, nonviolent technologies—Pottery, Alphabet, Code of Laws, and so on—are fairly safe trades. Always consult the research tree, however, to make sure that what you're trading doesn't give your opponent access to a Wonder you want to build or a head start on a military unit that poses a threat to your security.

When possible, avoid trading advances altogether, especially when you have a significant scientific advantage. Instead, offer to trade maps, luxury resources, or even cold hard cash for *their* advances. That way, you expand your knowledge without giving their research effort a boost.

CAUTION

It's dangerous to trade an advance that allows your opponent to upgrade his or her military capabilities. Chivalry and Gunpowder are two prime examples. Trade such an advance only if you are *positive* that the opponent doesn't have access to the strategic resources needed to build the military unit the advance allows. (As far as Chivalry is concerned, remember that the Indians don't need Horses to build their War Elephant units!)

Trade Cities? Are You Crazy?

The ability to trade cities is of limited use as far as bettering your own position. In practice, your opponents seldom (if ever) agree to a trade that involves surrendering a city to you.

Don't trade away your own cities except in certain, very specific circumstances. If a hostile rival hopelessly outmatches you and they won't sign a treaty with you no matter what other items you offer them, a city might appease them. Don't consider this last-resort tactic unless you're going to be overrun anyway.

Also consider trading away a city when the city in question is a "deadbeat"—a city that's not producing resources no matter what you do to improve the situation. (This is common among cities that you capture or assimilate.) If the city is doing you no good, give it to a rival and let him or her deal with the problem. He or she will love you for giving up the city, no matter how lame it is.

TIP

If you want to go to war with someone, but you don't want to take the reputation hit for initiating hostilities, enter trade negotiations with the rival in question and repeatedly ask them to give you a city. He or she might brush you off at first, but eventually become angry enough to declare war on you. Then, you can smite back in self-defense with no consequences to your reputation.

DIPLOMATIC ACTIONS AND ESPIONAGE

Your dealings with other civilizations don't have to take place on the battlefield or over the negotiating table. At times you want to take action against an opponent without ever facing him or her. That's where diplomatic actions and espionage come in.

NOTE

The methods of performing diplomatic actions and espionage have changed considerably in *Civilization III*. Veteran players should peruse this section for helpful tips on the new covert action rules.

Diplomatic Actions

As soon as you establish an embassy with a foreign power, you can start using it. At first, your options are limited. You can use the embassy to contact the civilization's leader (which you can do in other ways as well). The other two options are a little more interesting, however.

Investigate City

This option allows you to take a peek inside any of your rival's cities to see the population, current production project, garrisoned units, and so on—anything you can see when you look at your own city display. You can do this at any time with little fear of being caught. It's a great way to scope out an enemy before you launch an invasion.

Another, more scrupulous, method of using a spy to investigate a city is to save first, then scope out the city carefully. When you're finished, return to your previous save. Your spy is not lost and can scope that same city again later or perform other actions.

Steal Technology

By exercising this option, you instruct your diplomat to steal a random advance (that you haven't yet researched) from your rival. This activity is pricey in more ways than one. First, your chance of success depends on how much Gold you're willing to spend.

Spending more Gold gives you a better chance. (The average chance of success is about 75 percent.) Second, if you get caught, this is considered an act of war.

Stealing an advance from a rival is risky business and shouldn't be attempted if you want to maintain peaceful relations.

> **NOTE**
>
> No diplomatic actions are possible against civilizations you are at war with. Your embassy is closed for the duration of the conflict—if no spy is present in the embassy. If a spy is present, the flow of information is uninterrupted.

Espionage Actions

After you research Espionage (and build the Intelligence Agency Small Wonder) you can engage in a wider array of covert activities in empires where you have established an embassy.

To engage in these activities, you must first plant a spy in the embassy. This operation has about a 50 percent chance of success, so don't undertake it lightly. If your attempt to plant a spy fails, you've made an instant enemy of the victim civilization. Don't attempt espionage against any civilization you want to remain friendly with.

Assuming you're willing to take the risk to implant the spy and you are successful in doing so, a wide variety of nefarious options become available when you access your embassy.

> **NOTE**
>
> Under Communism, your spies are more experienced at their duties. Therefore, all espionage attempts under Communism have a slightly better chance of succeeding.

Espionage Activities

Spies carry out the following activities:

- **Sabotage:** If successful, the spy destroys the unit, improvement, or Wonder currently being produced in the selected city. This is a great way to keep your rivals from building a Wonder that you want.

- **Propaganda:** This is an attempt to get a target city to defect to your civilization. The chances vary widely depending on the Culture Point ratio between your empire and theirs (see table 5-4).

When the same city is subjected to ensuing propaganda campaigns, their resistance diminishes somewhat. The chances of successfully launching a propaganda campaign are shown in table 5-6. The chances of the target civilization resisting said campaign are shown in table 5-7. These factors are *further* modified based on the governments of the attacker and the defender. (More advanced governments resist propaganda more efficiently, especially when launched by less advanced governments.)

NOTE

Cities under Anarchy are immune to propaganda.

- **Steal Plans:** A useful activity to attempt before you launch an attack, this action reveals the position of all of your opponent's military units on the Military Advisor's mini-map for the remainder of the current turn. Move your cursor over any unit on the Advisor's screen for the affected civilization to reveal its position.

- **Steal World Map:** Reveals all the territory that the rival has explored. In most cases, it's simpler (and far less risky) to simply trade for your opponent's map.

- **Expose Spy:** Recalls your spy back to your capital to expose an enemy spy (if there is one). This mission is the best reason for having a spy; enemy spies can damage you as much as your spies damage them.

NOTE

The chance of success for each espionage activity (with the exception of propaganda) is complicated. The average rate of success for each is about 75 percent. This does *not* indicate the chance of your spy being caught in the act—that can happen whether the spy is successful or not. If your spy is caught, any of these activities is considered an act of war.

TABLE 5-6.
CHANCE FOR PROPAGANDA SUCCESS

TARGET IS:	CHANCE FOR SUCCESS
In awe of attacker	30%
An admirer of attacker	25%
Impressed with attacker	20%
Unimpressed with attacker	10%
Dismissive of attacker	5%
Disdainful of attacker	3%

TABLE 5-7. CHANCE TO RESIST PROPAGANDA

TARGET IS:	INITIAL CHANCE TO RESIST	CONTINUED CHANCE TO RESIST
In awe of attacker	40%	30%
An admirer of attacker	50%	40%
Impressed with attacker	60%	50%
Unimpressed with attacker	70%	60%
Dismissive of attacker	80%	70%
Disdainful of attacker	90%	80%

TIP

In most cases, it's easier to win over an opponent's city by building up your Culture. When your Culture is sufficiently better than theirs, your rival's cities will start defecting to your empire without your having to resort to propaganda.

THE GOLDEN AGE

The Golden Age can occur once every game. It's usually triggered when your civilization's unique military unit wins a battle for the first time, but it can also be triggered when you build the right combination of Wonders (see the Civilopedia for details).

This has major implications for your empire as a whole because, during the Golden Age, your resource output goes through the roof. Every terrain square in your empire produces one extra unit of each of the big three resources: food, shields, and commerce. The effects of the Golden Age continue for 20 turns.

It's important to plan for your Golden Age if at all possible. Although it's beneficial at any time during the game, it is *more* useful if your empire is large. The more cities you have, the more resources you'll reap as a result of the increased terrain productivity.

If you can, avoid triggering the Golden Age until you have 10 or more cities and a high rate of resource production. Obviously, it's easier to wait if your civilization's unit appears late in the game. The Americans, with their F-15 unit that doesn't appear until Modern Times, stand to reap the highest rewards from their Golden Age, while the Aztecs, with their Jaguar Warriors, have little hope of defeating an enemy beyond Ancient Times.

THE ADVANCE OF KNOWLEDGE

Throughout the history of the world, one of the driving forces behind humankind's development has been the quest for knowledge. New developments in sociological and scientific fields are the cornerstones of every advanced civilization, in the game as well as in the real world.

The *Civilization® III* game is one of many fabrics, all of which are important pieces of a complex tapestry. However, if you had to point to one element that is most important, it would have to be research. The discovery of new civilization advances is central to every other element of the game. If you fall behind in your research efforts, your opponents will make quick work of you and your primitive society, ending your game

quickly. Make a bad decision and head down the wrong research path and you could be left behind militarily or technologically, leaving the road to victory wide open for your opponents.

This chapter is dedicated entirely to research. In the first section, you'll learn how the research system works and what you can do to optimize your scientific efforts. The second portion of the chapter takes you on an age-by-age tour of all of the civilization advances, providing a complete description of the benefits of each. Finally, you'll be introduced to some basic research strategies that will help you follow the research path that best suits your needs and style of play.

SCIENCE 101

You start each game with two civilization advances. The advances vary depending on which civilization you're playing (see chapter II for details), but they're always two of the five basic advances in Ancient Times. To grow beyond this basic level of knowledge, you must build a city and start accumulating commerce. Within a turn or two of building your first city, you'll be asked to select the first advance you'd like to research.

The speed at which you research civilization advances is primarily determined by the amount of commerce that your empire is producing. As discussed in chapter III, commerce is divided into taxes, luxuries, and science. At the start of every turn, commerce is totaled and divided based on the percentages you've set on the Domestic Advisor's screen.

The number of science icons your empire generates each turn is applied to the current research project. Each advance has a set research cost. When enough science icons accumulate, the advance is discovered and you are prompted to select the next research project. The Science Advisor's screen shows you the number

of turns it will take to research any given advance based on the amount of research your empire is generating. Research projects become progressively pricier as you go through the game.

In *Civilization III*, research is clearly divided into four ages of development—Ancient Times, Middle Ages, Industrial Ages, and Modern Times. Although you don't have to research every advance in a given age to move on to the next age, you *do* have to research most of them. The advance descriptions later in this chapter reveal which technologies you can skip and still progress to the next age.

Maximizing Your Research Capabilities

Every city you build generates *some* commerce, so you can carry out research simply by allocating some of that commerce to science. Of course, there are ways to improve your science capacity.

Adjust Your Commerce Levels

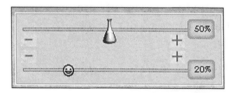

The most obvious way to increase your empire's science output is by increasing the percentage of commerce that is dedicated to scientific research—the higher the

percentage, the faster your research. This is actually one of the only courses of action available to you early in the game, and it's an excellent way to give your science an early boost.

After you build your first city, visit the Domestic Advisor's screen and set your science as high as you can—90 percent is the maximum. Until your empire starts to grow, you don't have a pressing need for tax income, and the citizens (the first few, anyway) are content without your having to allocate any commerce to luxuries.

Keep an eye on your treasury. As soon as it starts to dwindle (due to unit support and improvement maintenance) readjust your commerce levels to compensate. On the higher difficulty levels, also watch your population's attitude, and be prepared to compensate when unhappy citizens are "born" in your growing cities. In any case, you should be able to keep the science flowing for quite a while before it becomes a problem.

Later in the game, when terrain-generated luxuries and happiness- and tax-generating improvements are in place, use this tactic again to generate extra science.

Build Cities in Commerce-Rich Areas

Because science is a component of commerce, the more commerce your empire generates, the higher its potential science output. Coast and Sea are the only terrain types

that generate commerce by default, but you can remedy this by having your Workers build roads on every available square within the city radius. Every terrain type (except Ocean, Sea, and Coast, of course) generates one unit of commerce when it's improved with a road.

Also, be on the lookout for special resources that increase commerce. Gold is one of the best but, if possible, look for strategic or luxury resources. That way, the resource increases your commerce *and* provides either a valuable component for the construction of units and improvements or a source of happiness for your population.

TIP

Luxury resources—Silk and Gems in particular—are excellent double-duty resources when you want a city to produce more commerce (and, ultimately, more science). They provide a significant amount of commerce, and the presence of the luxury items allows you to channel some of your luxury commerce into science without affecting your citizens' happiness.

Improvements and Wonders

You can build a number of improvements and Wonders to increase your cities' research output. The more of these structures that you have in place, the faster your research progresses. Table 6-1 lists the science-enhancing improvements and Wonders and their effects.

TABLE 6-1. RESEARCH-ENHANCING IMPROVEMENTS AND WONDERS

IMPROVEMENT/WONDER	EFFECT
IMPROVEMENTS	
Library	Increases the city's science output by 50%
Research Lab	Increases the city's science output by 50% (cumulative with Library and University).
University	Increases the city's science output by 50% (cumulative with Library).
WONDERS	
Copernicus's Observatory	Increases city's science output by 100% (cumulative with existing improvements and Wonders).
Newton's University	Increases city's science output by 100% (cumulative with existing improvements and Wonders).
SETI Program	Doubles science in the city where it's built (cumulative with existing improvements and Wonders).
The Great Library	Automatically gives you any advance already discovered by at least two other civilizations.
Theory of Evolution	Grants two automatic civilization advances.

NOTE

The Colossus, which increases commerce, also bolsters your science effort, though less directly than the science-specific improvements and Wonders.

Convert Citizens into Scientists

As described in chapter IV, you can relieve your citizens of their resource-gathering duties and convert them into specialists. Just as Entertainers increase population happiness and tax collectors increase tax

income, scientists improve the city's science output. Every scientist you create generates additional science icons in that city.

Creating a scientist is a double-edged sword, especially in a small city. Every citizen you remove from resource-gathering duties decreases the city's resource base. This can lead to stagnation and slow production in that city. In fact, if the citizen you convert was working a terrain square that generated a lot of commerce, turning that citizen into a scientist could be counterproductive. Make sure the commerce you lose doesn't equal or outweigh the science you gain.

NOTE

Veteran players should note that a city no longer needs a population of five or more before you can create a scientist. Scientists can now be created in cities of any size.

Switch Governments

One final way of increasing commerce—and, hence, science—is by choosing a form of government that is conducive to free trade. As a general rule, commerce output increases as government types become more advanced. The governments' effect on corruption also has a bearing on this decision—the more corruption you experience, the less commerce you have to devote to science.

Government commerce output (from lowest to highest) is:

- Despotism
- Monarchy
- Communism
- Republic
- Democracy

THE CIVILIZATION ADVANCES

A frequently occurring questions is "What do I research next?" You *can* simply follow the Research Advisor's advice, or you can pick advances at random—but that often leads to undesirable results. It's always best to have a plan and, to plan effectively, you need to know the benefits of researching one advance over another. Analyze your situation and decide what advance best suits your needs and your strategy.

Civilization III divides the advances into four distinct ages, and this chapter explores the advances on an age-by-age basis. Table 6-2 consolidates all of the advances into a single, alphabetical table so you can quickly reference the vital statistics of any advance. The following information is listed for each advance:

- **Prerequisites:** The earlier advance(s) you must discover before you can research the advance.
- **Units:** The units that you can produce after you research the advance.

- **Improvements:** The city improvements you can build after you research the advance.
- **Wonders:** The Wonders of the World and Small Wonders that you can produce after you research the advance.
- **Advances Allowed:** The new advances you can research after you research the advance.

TABLE 6-2. CIVILIZATION ADVANCES AT A GLANCE

ADVANCE	PREREQUISITES	UNITS	IMPROVEMENTS	WONDERS	ADVANCES ALLOWED
Advanced Flight	Flight, Radio, Motorized Transportation	Helicopter, Paratrooper	—	—	—
Alphabet	—	—	—	—	Mathematics, Writing
Amphibious War	Mass Production	Marine	—	—	—
Astronomy	Education	Caravel	—	Copernicus's Observatory	Navigation, Physics
Atomic Theory	Scientific Method	—	—	—	Electronics
Banking	Education	—	Bank	—	Democracy, Economics
Bronze Working	—	Spearman, Hoplite, Impi	—	The Colossus	Iron Working
Ceremonial Burial	—	—	Temple	—	Mysticism
Chemistry	Gunpowder	—	—	—	Metallurgy, Physics
Chivalry	Monotheism, Feudalism	Knight, Samurai, War Elephant	—	—	—
Code of Laws	Writing	—	Courthouse	—	The Republic
Combustion	Refining, Steel	Destroyer, Transport	—	—	Flight, Mass Production
Communism	Nationalism	—	Police Station	—	—

continued on next page

TABLE 6-2. CIVILIZATION ADVANCES AT A GLANCE, CONTINUED

ADVANCE	PREREQUISITES	UNITS	IMPROVEMENTS	WONDERS	ADVANCES ALLOWED
Computers	—	Mech Infantry	Research Lab	SETI Program	Miniaturization, The Laser
Construction	Iron Working, Mathematics	—	Aqueduct, Colosseum	The Great Wall	—
The Corporation	Industrialization	—	—	—	Refining, Steel
Currency	Mathematics	—	Marketplace	—	—
Democracy	Printing Press, Banking	—	—	—	Free Artistry
Ecology	—	—	Mass Transit System, Solar Plant	—	—
Economics	Banking	—	—	Smith's Trading Company	—
Education	Theology	—	University	—	Astronomy, Banking, Music Theory
Electricity	Steam Power	—	—	—	Replaceable Parts, Scientific Method
Electronics	Atomic Theory	—	Hydro Plant	Hoover Dam	Motorized Transportation, Radio
Engineering	—	—	—	—	Invention
Espionage	Nationalism, Industrialization	—	—	Intelligence Agency	—
Feudalism	—	Pikeman, Rider	—	Sun Tzu's Art of War	Chivalry, Invention
Fission	—	Nuclear Submarine	—	The Manhattan Project, The United Nations	Nuclear Power, Superconductor
Flight	Combustion	Bomber, Fighter	Airport	—	Advanced Flight
Free Artistry	Democracy	—	—	Shakespeare's Theater	—

continued on next page

TABLE 6-2. CIVILIZATION ADVANCES AT A GLANCE, CONTINUED

ADVANCE	PREREQUISITES	UNITS	IMPROVEMENTS	WONDERS	ADVANCES ALLOWED
Genetics	Miniaturization	—	—	Cure for Cancer, Longevity	—
Gunpowder	Invention	Musketman, Musketeer	—	—	Chemistry
Horseback Riding	The Wheel, Warrior Code	Horseman, Mounted Warrior	—	—	—
Industrialization	Steam Power	—	Coal Plant, Factory	Universal Suffrage	Espionage, The Corporation
Integrated Defense	Superconductor, Satellites, Smart Weapons	—	—	Strategic Missile Defense	—
Invention	Feudalism, Engineering	Longbowman	—	Leonardo's Workshop	Gunpowder
Iron Working	Bronze Working	Swordsman, Immortals, Legionary	—	—	Construction
The Laser	Nuclear Power, Computers	—	SS Planetary Party Lounge	—	Robotics, Smart Weapons
Literature	Writing	—	Library	The Great Library	—
Magnetism	Physics	Frigate, Galleon, Privateer, Man-O-War	—	—	—
Map Making	Writing, Pottery	Galley	Harbor	The Great Lighthouse	—
Masonry	—	—	Palace, Walls	The Pyramids	Mathematics
Mass Production	Combustion, Replaceable Parts	Battleship, Carrier, Submarine	—	—	Amphibious War, Motorized Transportation
Mathematics	Masonry, Alphabet	Catapult	—	—	Construction, Currency

continued on next page

TABLE 6-2. CIVILIZATION ADVANCES AT A GLANCE, CONTINUED

ADVANCE	PREREQUISITES	UNITS	IMPROVEMENTS	WONDERS	ADVANCES ALLOWED
Medicine	—	—	—	—	Sanitation, Scientific Method
Metallurgy	Chemistry	Cannon	Coastal Fortress	—	Military Tradition
Military Tradition	Metallurgy	Cavalry, Cossack	—	Military Academy	—
Miniaturization	Computers	—	Offshore Platform	—	Genetics, Robotics
Monarchy	Warrior Code, Polytheism	—	—	The Hanging Gardens	—
Monotheism	—	—	Cathedral	—	Chivalry, Theology
Motorized Transportation	Mass Production, Electronics	Tank, Panzer	—	—	Advanced Flight
Music Theory	Education	—	—	JS Bach's Cathedral	—
Mysticism	Ceremonial Burial	—	—	The Oracle	Polytheism
Nationalism	—	Rifleman	—	—	Communism, Espionage
Navigation	Astronomy	Explorer	—	Magellan's Voyage	—
Nuclear Power	Fission	—	Nuclear Plant	—	The Laser
Philosophy	Writing	—	—	—	The Republic
Physics	Astronomy, Chemistry	—	—	—	Magnetism, Theory of Gravity
Polytheism	Mysticism	—	—	—	Monarchy
Pottery	—	—	Granary	—	Map Making
Printing Press	Theology	—	—	—	Democracy
Radio	Electronics	—	—	—	Advanced Flight
Recycling	Ecology	—	Recycling Center	—	Synthetic Fibers

continued on next page

TABLE 6-2. CIVILIZATION ADVANCES AT A GLANCE, CONTINUED

ADVANCE	PREREQUISITES	UNITS	IMPROVEMENTS	WONDERS	ADVANCES ALLOWED
Refining	The Corporation	—	—	—	Combustion
Replaceable Parts	Electricity	Artillery, Infantry	—	—	Mass Production
The Republic	Philosophy, Code of Laws	—	—	—	—
Robotics	The Laser, Miniaturization	AEGIS Cruiser, Radar Artillery	Manufacturing Plant	—	—
Rocketry	—	Cruise Missile, Jet Fighter, F-15	SAM Missile Battery	—	Space Flight
Sanitation	Medicine	—	Hospital	—	—
Satellites	Space Flight	ICBM	SS Thrusters	Integrated Defense, Smart Weapons	—
Scientific Method	Medicine, Electricity	—	—	Theory of Evolution	Atomic Theory
Smart Weapons	Satellites, The Laser	—	—	—	Integrated Defense
Space Flight	Rocketry	Tactical Nuke	SS Cockpit, SS Docking Bay, SS Engine	Apollo Program	Satellites, Superconductor
Stealth	Synthetic Fibers	Stealth Bomber, Stealth Fighter	—	—	—
Steam Power	—	Ironclad	—	—	Electricity, Industrialization
Steel	The Corporation	—	—	—	Combustion
Superconductor	Fission, Space Flight	—	SS Fuel Cells, SS Life Support System	—	Integrated Defense
Synthetic Fibers	Recycling	Modern Armor	SS Exterior Casing, SS Stasis Chamber, SS Storage/Supply	—	Stealth

continued on next page

TABLE 6-2. CIVILIZATION ADVANCES AT A GLANCE, CONTINUED

ADVANCE	PREREQUISITES	UNITS	IMPROVEMENTS	WONDERS	ADVANCES ALLOWED
Theology	Monotheism	—	—	Sistine Chapel	Education, Printing Press
Warrior Code	—	Archer, Bowman	—	—	Horseback Riding, Monarchy
The Wheel	—	Chariot, War Chariot	—	—	Horseback Riding
Writing	Alphabet	—	—	—	Code of Laws, Literature, Map Making, Philosophy

NOTE

The advances at the start of each age are listed as having no prerequisites. That's not exactly true. To research these advances, you must progress past the previous age. For example, to research Computers, you must first discover all of the required advances in the Industrial Age.

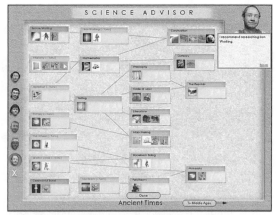

The research tree for Ancient Times

Ancient Advances

The advances in Ancient Times are the cornerstones for all of your future technologies. They're the least "expensive" to research—but, then again, you have fewer science resources available at this point in the game.

To begin research on Middle Ages advances, you must research all of the Ancient Times advances *except:*

- Horseback Riding
- Literature
- Monarchy
- Republic

Alphabet

The importance of the Alphabet isn't readily apparent because it provides you with no immediate units, improvements, or Wonders. But, like so many of the game's advances, the long-term benefits of the Alphabet make it important to pursue at your earliest convenience. This advance is the first rung on the intellectual ladder that leads to important discoveries such as Mathematics and Literature.

Bronze Working

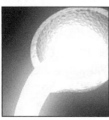

Bronze Working is the first military advance available. Many civilizations start the game with this advance, but if yours isn't one of them, make Bronze Working your first research project of the game. Depending on Warriors to defend your cities can make for a very short game. Bronze Working is also the first step along the path that leads to Construction (Colosseums, Aqueducts, and The Great Wall).

Ceremonial Burial

After you get your early military needs out of the way with Bronze Working, think about keeping your population happy. Ceremonial Burial, which allows you to build Temples, the first of the "happiness" improvements, should be high on your list (if you didn't start the game with it, that is). The higher the difficulty level, the more important it is to research this advance early. At higher difficulty levels, you need to pacify your population early on. And Ceremonial Burial is the first step toward an advanced form of government (Monarchy).

Code of Laws

Code of Laws is an important advance for two reasons: Courthouses and The Republic. In the short term, Courthouses help reduce the rampant corruption and waste under Despotism.

In the long term, this is one of the two prerequisite advances (along with Philosophy) that allow you to research The Republic, arguably the second best government available in the game. If you're following any nonviolent strategy, head down this path as soon as possible so you can switch to a Republic.

Construction

Construction is one of the most significant advances of Ancient Times. By far the most important benefit of this advance is the ability to build Aqueducts. Without them, your cities stop growing. If you have problems with population unhappiness, reach Construction as quickly as possible so that you can reap the benefits of the Colosseum.

Currency

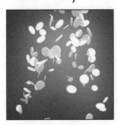

Currency is one of the few Ancient advances you can afford to put on the back burner for a while in favor of other, more pressing matters. While the Marketplace improvement is very useful for increasing commerce (and, hence, science, luxuries, and taxes), its effects are less important than those of Libraries (Literature) and the two advanced forms of government. You

can always come back to this advance at a later time if need be. In fact, you have to—you can't get to the Middle Ages without it!

Horseback Riding

Horseback Riding is one of the four "skippable" Ancient advances, but there are two very good reasons not to skip it— especially if you're following a military strategy. First, it allows you to build Horsemen, the most mobile military units of Ancient Times. It also makes the Horses strategic resource appear on the map. Without Horses, you can't build the important Knight and Cavalry units that are such a mainstay of your military during the Middle Ages. Although you can safely put this advance off if there is no immediate military need for it, don't let it fall by the wayside when you advance to the next age.

Iron Working

Just as Bronze Working provides your first effective defensive unit, Iron Working provides your first effective offensive unit—the Swordsman. Research this important advance early if you're building up your offensive forces for an early rout of a neighboring civilization. However, if you have no pressing need for a strong attacker, put Iron Working aside in favor of intellectual pursuits such as Alphabet or spiritual pursuits such as Ceremonial Burial. Come back to this line of research when you need a strong military or are ready to make a run for Construction.

Literature

Early discovery of Literature is important to both military and nonmilitary strategies. For the pacifist, this advance offers the scientific benefits of the Library, which gives your early research efforts a boost. For you warmongers, building the Great Library is a great way to compensate for the lagging research that often accompanies a militant strategy—the free advances help you keep up with your enemies in the research race.

TIP

Although the game allows you to skip Literature and still move on to the Middle Ages, don't even consider letting this important advance slip through the cracks. If you do, the impact on your ongoing research efforts could be devastating.

Map Making

In the previous incarnations of *Civilization,* the importance of Map Making was primarily tied to your dependence on naval units for exploration early in the game. While this is still true, Map Making now has a more important purpose: Harbors. Harbors are an integral part of your trade network, allowing you to share strategic and luxury resources with cities that can't be connected to your empire by roads. If you are playing on a world where your cities are likely to be separated by water, make Map Making a priority so you can get your Harbors up and running early in the game.

NOTE

Another new bonus provided by Map Making is the ability to trade maps with other civilizations during trade negotiations. This makes exploring the world a lot easier.

Masonry

After Bronze Working and Ceremonial Burial, Masonry is your next best early-game research choice. It provides immediate benefits for growth (The Pyramids) and defense (Walls). It is also a key advance in the research path that leads to both Currency and Construction (through Mathematics). Unless you need the immediate offensive benefits of Iron Working or Warrior Code, Masonry should be no later than third on your research "to do" list.

Mathematics

The immediate benefit of Mathematics is offensive in nature: namely, the ability to build Catapults. The more important benefits of Mathematics, however, are the research opportunities it opens up—Currency and, more importantly, Construction. While Writing and Mysticism should take precedence unless you have a pressing need for Catapults, don't put Mathematics off for too long.

Monarchy

Monarchy is one of the two alternatives to Despotism available in Ancient Times (the other being The Republic). You *must* get away from Despotism as soon as possible to maximize your empire's resources. Whether you choose Monarchy or Republic depends on your ultimate goal. Monarchy is the better choice if you're following a warlike strategy—you won't have to worry about war weariness, and many advances that lead up to Monarchy are military in nature.

TIP

Monarchy is one of the skippable advances of Ancient Times, but don't skip it even if you never intend to govern by Monarchy. The Hanging Gardens, a major "happiness" Wonder that used to be available when you researched Pottery, is now available through Monarchy. If you want to build The Hanging Gardens, you've got to fit Monarchy into your busy research schedule.

Mysticism

The most obvious benefit of Mysticism is The Oracle. In situations where your citizens' happiness is hanging in the balance, Mysticism is a very important advance indeed. The Oracle can be of great assistance in preventing civil disorder early in the game. Of all the second-tier Ancient advances, only Writing is more important. Mysticism gains a slight priority over Writing if you're making a run for Monarchy.

Philosophy

Philosophy is a crucial link in the chain of advances leading to The Republic. By the time this advance comes up for research, you've probably got a lot of choices available. Because Philosophy offers no immediate benefits, Literature and Code of Laws should take precedence in most cases. Don't put off Philosophy for too long if you've decided to pursue The Republic. Otherwise, Despotism will take its toll on your growing empire.

NOTE

The "free advance" bonus imparted to the first civilization to discover Philosophy in the previous *Civ* games doesn't exist in *Civilization III*. That means there's no big rush to be the first to discover this advance.

Polytheism

Polytheism is merely a stepping stone advance on the path to Monarchy. It provides no units, improvements, or Wonders, and has no other effect on your empire as a whole. Unless you are on a quest to discover Monarchy as soon as possible, put off this third-tier advance in favor of more lucrative advances such as Literature and Construction. Of course, you have to get around to it eventually— otherwise you can't advance to the Middle Ages!

Pottery

Pottery's immediate benefit is the Granary. As discussed in chapter VII, the benefit Granaries provide early in the game is debatable. Pottery only leads to one other advance—Map Making. So, the importance of Pottery is a rather subjective

thing. In most cases, you can put it off in favor of more important first-tier advances.

The Republic

The Republic is one of the two most advanced governments available in the game and, as such, is a very important milestone indeed. All of the advances that lead up to The Republic are scientific in nature. This, combined with the benefits of ruling a peaceful empire under this form of government, make an early run for The Republic a desirable course of action.

> **TIP**
>
> *Like Monarchy, The Republic is one of the skippable advances in Ancient Times. If you never intend to switch to this form of government—as is often the case when you pursue a warlike strategy—you can safely skip this advance and move on to the Middle Ages when you get the chance. Other than the government itself, The Republic advance provides no benefits whatsoever.*

Warrior Code

Warrior Code provides an obvious military benefit in the form of Archers. More importantly, however, this advance is one of the prerequisites for Horseback Riding and Monarchy. Because Spearmen are better defensive units than Archers, always put Bronze Working ahead of Warrior Code regardless of your ultimate strategy. Warrior Code makes an acceptable second research choice for a military strategy or when Barbarians or pesky neighboring civilizations rear their heads early in the game. Otherwise, put this advance aside for a while, at least until you research Alphabet and Ceremonial Burial.

The Wheel

Like Warrior Code, The Wheel provides you with an early offensive unit (the Chariot, in this case) and is a prerequisite to Horseback Riding. When you're deciding between the two, assess your needs and decide which unit you'd like to have first. Archers and Chariots share the same attack capabilities, but the more expensive Chariot has better movement *and* the ability to retreat.

If you don't need to field offensive units at all, The Wheel and Warrior Code are interchangeable.

Writing

When you glance at the research tree, it seems as if Writing provides you with no immediate benefits. While it is true that, like Alphabet, no units, improvements, or Wonders are made available by this advance, Writing *does* allow you to make treaties with rival civilizations. This is an important diplomatic skill—absolutely *vital* if you're out to make friends with your neighbors rather than conquering them.

More importantly, Writing allows three major advances—Literature, Code of Laws, and Map Making— and is one of the key steps on the path to The Republic. This advance should be high on your priority list, especially if you're following a nonmilitaristic strategy.

Middle Ages Advances

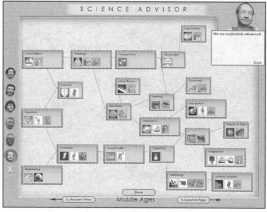

The research tree for the Middle Ages

In the Middle Ages, technologies advance beyond the basics. Many of the advances in the Middle Ages deal with the finer details of civilization, such as art, music, and finance. With the increase in technological sophistication comes a higher research price. If your cities' science output is less than adequate, this is where you'll start to feel it.

To begin research on Industrial Age advances, you must research all of the Middle Ages advances *except:*

- Chivalry
- Democracy
- Economics
- Free Artistry
- Military Tradition
- Music Theory
- Navigation
- Printing Press

Astronomy

Astronomy provides both immediate and long-term benefits. If you're doing a lot of exploring and traveling by sea, the Caravel unit, which Astronomy makes possible, is an important addition to your fleet. Astronomy also serves as a prerequisite to Navigation, which further enhances your seagoing capabilities.

Even if sea travel doesn't figure heavily in your strategy, the benefits of Copernicus's Observatory make Astronomy worthwhile. Building this Wonder assists in all of your future research endeavors.

NOTE

In addition to its obvious effects, Astronomy also allows trade to take place over Sea squares. (See chapter V for details on trade.)

Banking

Banking is a part of the intricate web of advances that leads to Democracy, the most advanced form of government in the game and the best available if your strategy is a peaceful one. When you figure in the Bank, an improvement that

boosts your tax revenues, the benefits of this advance are clear.

That said, if your goal is conquest, put off Banking in favor of the military advances in the Engineering–Military Tradition branch of the Middle Ages research tree. After you can build the units you need, go back and research Banking so you can build Banks to help support them.

TIP

For a real boost in your tax revenues over the entire game, build Banks in at least five of your cities and then construct the Wall Street Small Wonder. (See chapter VII for details.)

Chemistry

The military implications of Chemistry are obvious when you look at the research tree—you can't get to Metallurgy and Military Tradition without it. When you're on the warpath, you want to make a quick dash down this military branch of the tree, making Chemistry an important stop along the way.

If you're making a run for Democracy, jump down to Chemistry as soon as you can. Chemistry is a key advance that eventually leads to Theory of Gravity (Newton's University) and Magnetism (Galleons).

Chivalry

It's easy to overlook Chivalry in your rush to get to enticing advances such as Gunpowder and Democracy. This advance sits out there on its own at the beginning of the Middle Ages. You can skip this advance and still move on to the Industrial Ages, especially if you're in no danger from your neighbors and you aren't waging a war.

If you're in the middle of war, however, definitely do *not* ignore Chivalry. The best military units in the early Middle Ages are Knights, and you can't build them without Chivalry.

TIP

If you're playing as the Indians or the Japanese, never skip Chivalry. Without it you can't get the tribe-specific units available to these civilizations.

Democracy

Democracy is the pinnacle of government advancement. If you follow a peaceful strategy, make a run for Democracy as soon as you get to the Middle Ages. Your empire benefits from being a Democracy, and you pick up key scientific and religious advances along the way.

Democratic government can be problematical if conquest is your goal—it takes an experienced player to deal with the war weariness experienced by a Democracy at war. Military players can safely skip Democracy altogether. You can always come back to it later if you change your mind.

Economics

Economics is one of the Middle Ages' optional advances. Whether or not you should bother with Economics depends on how much you need the maintenance-saving benefits of Smith's Trading Company, which is the only benefit of researching this advance under normal circumstances. If your empire is economically sound and you don't plan to build the Wonder anyway, skip Economics for now and come back to it later.

TIP

Economics has one additional benefit: it doubles the shields-to-Gold exchange rate when you set a city to "build" Wealth. If you use this fund-raising method often, consider researching Economics.

Education

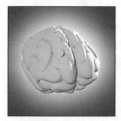

Education is an offshoot of Theology that forms its own sub-branch of the Middle Ages research tree. It's the advance that merges the military branch (Engineering–Military Tradition) and the peaceful branch (Monotheism-Democracy) forming a technological branch that leads to a number of key advances.

In addition to being the first step toward the advanced naval capabilities of Astronomy, Navigation, and Magnetism, Education offers the immediate ability to build Universities, the second of the three major science improvements. No matter what overall strategy you prefer, get education out of the way early, if only for the research boost it allows.

Engineering

The immediate benefits of Engineering are subtle. After you've discovered this advance, your Workers can build roads that span rivers, as well as plant forests. While both benefits are useful, they're not as important as the long-term benefits.

This advance, along with Feudalism, is the first step down the military branch of the Middle Ages research tree. It is also the

precursor to Invention (and, hence, Leonardo's Workshop), a useful Wonder no matter how you choose to play.

Even so, Engineering should *not* be among your first research choices in the Middle Ages. Research Monotheism, Feudalism, and Chivalry before you consider this advance.

Feudalism

Feudalism is the best advance to pursue upon entering the Middle Ages. This advance allows you to build Pikemen, the first effective defenders of the new age. Feudalism also allows you to build Sun Tzu's Art of War, which is a boon to any aggressive strategy.

If you are experiencing happiness problems, however, your first choice should be Monotheism.

Free Artistry

This offshoot of Democracy is one of the Middle Ages' optional advances. It usually becomes available near the end of the age (depending on your research strategy), around the same time as a number of pivotal late–Middle Ages advances.

While just about any advance takes precedence over Free Artistry, don't skip it entirely. The happiness benefits of Shakespeare's Theater are worth the research time.

> **NOTE**
>
> If one of your opponents builds Shakespeare's Theater before you research Free Artistry, there's no need to research this advance.

Gunpowder

Gunpowder is a major turning point for military units. If you're following a conquest strategy, make a beeline for this (as soon as you've squared away the basics, such as Monotheism). Most military-oriented advances of the Middle Ages lie beyond Gunpowder.

The benefits of Gunpowder are also useful if you're going the peaceful route, because Musketmen are primarily defensive units. Research this advance if you think you'll be invaded in the near future.

Invention

Invention is a useful short-term research goal for aggressive and passive strategies alike. The reason? Leonardo's Workshop. Whether you're waging war on your neighbors or simply staving off the occasional invader, the half-price unit upgrades that this Wonder offers saves you a lot of shields and time.

Aggressive types can reap some benefit from the Longbowman unit that Invention makes possible, although Knights are the preferred attack unit of this era. Aside from Leonardo's Workshop, the real benefit of Invention is that it opens the door to most of the military advances of the Middle Ages.

Magnetism

Magnetism is *the* naval advance of the Middle Ages. Before this advance, your seafaring is limited to lowly Galleys and Caravels. After Magnetism, your choices include two warships (Frigates and Privateers) and a high-capacity transport (the Galleon). Magnetism also opens Ocean squares to trade (see chapter V for details).

If your strategy involves naval warfare or if you're on a world with a lot of water, make a run for Magnetism before you go for other military advances such as Metallurgy and Military Tradition.

Metallurgy

 This advance falls near the end of the military branch of the Middle Ages' research tree. It provides both a new bombardment weapon (the Cannon) and the useful Coastal Fortress city improvement. Cannons are useful only in aggressive scenarios, but Coastal Fortresses benefit any style of play.

Unless you're at war with another civilization, Metallurgy can be put off until after you researched some of the more immediately beneficial advances.

Military Tradition

 Military Tradition, as its name suggests, provides benefits that are entirely military in nature. Cavalry units are the most mobile and powerful attack units in the Middle Ages, and if they can be built early on, they can turn the tide of an ongoing war. But, to get to Military Tradition early in the Middle Ages,

you have to put off a lot of important nonmilitary advances along the way.

This is one of the optional advances of this age and, if you're not going to need the Military Academy or Cavalry units, there's no need to research it. Passive players can let this one slide.

TIP

Don't skip Military Tradition if you're playing as the Russians. Otherwise, you'll never be able to build your civ-specific unit, the Cossack.

Monotheism

 Monotheism is the first advance in the peaceful yet lucrative Middle Ages research branch that eventually leads to Democracy. This advance is the second one you should research when you reach the Middle Ages (right after Feudalism). No matter what sort of strategy you employ, the happiness benefits derived from Cathedrals are vital to your continued success. Even playing the military game, deviate from your normal research course long enough to grab this advance.

Music Theory

Music Theory is similar to Free Artistry in that it is a spur advance that leads nowhere but is too good to ignore because of the Wonder it allows you to build. It has the edge on Free Artistry when it comes to importance, though, because the happiness effects of JS Bach's Cathedral, though less dramatic, are more widespread.

Research this optional advance rather than skipping it—but only if nobody else has built JS Bach's Cathedral *and* you're willing to take the time to build the Wonder yourself.

Navigation

Navigation is another optional advance. If you're a fan of naval warfare and/or sea travel, Magellan's Voyage, which becomes available with this advance, gives you a definite mobility edge over your opponents.

Unless you want to build Magellan's Voyage, there's no good reason to research Navigation. The Explorer unit made possible by this advance is not compelling enough to divert your research from the many more advances available at this time.

NOTE

Navigation opens trade across Ocean squares, which is a valuable benefit. However, the same benefit becomes available when you research Magnetism, so it doesn't make Navigation any more appealing.

Physics

Physics, like Chemistry before it, is a link in the chain that leads to the end of the military branch of the Middle Ages' research tree. If you're making a push for naval superiority, choose Physics over Metallurgy when you're deciding where to go from Chemistry—assuming you've already researched Astronomy, of course. Otherwise, put this advance aside and finish out the two military advances (Metallurgy and Military Tradition) first.

Printing Press

Printing Press is the Chemistry of the nonaggressive branch of the Middle Ages research tree. It provides no benefits of its own, but it is one of the two immediate prerequisites of Democracy and, as such, vital to your research efforts if

the pinnacle of peacetime governments is your goal.

If Democracy's not your thing, there's no need to research this advance—you don't need it to advance to the Industrial Ages.

Theology

The second advance on the peaceful path in this age is important no matter how you choose to play. The immediate benefit of Theology, the Sistine Chapel, is a great happiness generator. But the main importance of this advance is that it allows you to research Education, which, in turn, leads to numerous important advances. Although you can safely put this advance off in favor of making a run for Gunpowder, come back to Theology soon thereafter.

Theory of Gravity

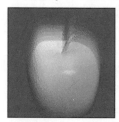

Theory of Gravity is an end-of-the-line advance in this age. Its major asset, Newton's University, is quite beneficial (though localized). Even so, it's better to have the Wonder to yourself rather than let one of your opponents reap its benefits. If you're on a peaceful track, give Theory of Gravity precedence over age-ending advances such as Magnetism.

If you need the benefits of military-oriented advances, you have to take a chance that no one will build Newton's University before you get back around to researching Theory of Gravity.

Industrial Ages Advances

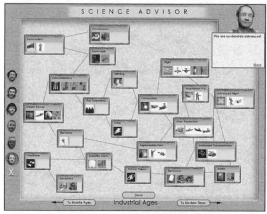

The research tree for the Industrial Ages

The dawn of the Industrial Ages brings great military and technological power. It also brings the problem of pollution, something that isn't easy to deal with until Modern Times. Again, the research prices jump over the previous age, making the optimization of your cities' science output crucial if you want to keep up with your opponents technologically.

The research "tree" in the Industrial Ages is more like a web and, as such, most of the advances must be researched in order to move on. To advance to Modern Times, you must research all Industrial Ages advances *except:*

- Advanced Flight
- Amphibious War
- Communism
- Espionage
- Nationalism
- Sanitation

Advanced Flight

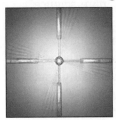

Advanced Flight is an optional end-of-the-era advance that provides a pair of unique units—Helicopters and Paratroopers. Both of these units are very specialized and might not appeal to everyone. Check out their statistics and abilities in chapter VIII to decide if these units suit your needs. If not, skip this advance. If they do appeal to you, decide when you need them and research this advance when the time is right to implement your strategy. In most cases, you should move on to Modern Times and come back to Advanced Flight when you need it.

Amphibious War

Like Advanced Flight, Amphibious War is an optional advance that provides specialized military power—in this case, the Marine unit. (See chapter VIII for details on this unit.) This technology primarily benefits the conquest-minded player. If you don't need Marines, don't bother with this advance.

Atomic Theory

Like The Corporation and Steel, Atomic Theory is simply a steppingstone advance. It doesn't offer anything of value in and of itself, but it is only one step away from Electronics, one of the most pivotal late Industrial advances. If you're out to conquer the world, this advance can take a temporary backseat to Combustion, Replaceable Parts, and Mass Production—but you must come back to it before you can get Tanks.

Combustion

The immediate benefits of Combustion are obvious—Destroyers to rule the seas and Transports to take the ground war to your distant enemies (or take your Settlers to distant continents— whichever you prefer). Despite its distinctly naval flavor, Combustion is a pivotal advance that leads to modern ground and air units as well.

Communism

Unlike Democracy and The Republic, don't skip Communism just because don't want to use it as a form of government. In addition to allowing Communist rule, this advance lets you build Police Stations, which are crucial if you're conducting a war under a Republic or a Democracy. Yes, you can skip Communism and still progress to Modern Times, and it's a low priority advance unless you want to rule through Communism. Just remember that Police Stations are a nice fallback option if your plans for peaceful victory go awry.

The Corporation

This is the first advance in the triumvirate that leads to Combustion and the first of the modern naval units (Destroyers and Transports). The Corporation offers nothing in the way of units, improvements, and Wonders—it's merely a necessary link in the military-oriented portion of the Industrial Ages' research chain.

Electricity

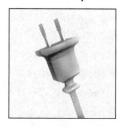

Electricity is the first of the "pure science" advances in the Industrial Age. It's the first step in the path that eventually leads to Radio. Despite the fact that it allows no new units, improvements, or Wonders, Electricity should be fairly high on your priority list regardless of your preferred strategy. It allows your Workers to irrigate from any water source—a real growth boost if many of your cities lack access to fresh water.

Electronics

Electronics offers the first shield-boosting alternatives to the pollution-belching Coal Plant—Hydro Plants and the Hoover Dam Wonder. Electronics is also a prerequisite for both Motorized Transportation and Radio. This advance truly has something for everyone.

Espionage

The value of researching Espionage, one of the Industrial Ages' optional technologies, depends on whether or not you like to wage a war of subversion rather than attacking your enemies in the open. Espionage allows you to build the Intelligence Agency Small Wonder, which, in turn, allows you to carry out spy missions. (See chapter V for details.) If spying isn't your thing, you can skip this advance altogether.

Flight

Flight might seem like a purely military advance because its most noticeable effect is that it ushers in the era of air units. Because of the new trade system in *Civ III*, Airports have a new importance— they allow the sharing of strategic and luxury resources between any of your cities equipped with Airports. This link is crucial as your empire spreads over a progressively larger area.

Before you make a beeline for Mass Production and Motorized Transportation, research Flight. That way, your distant cities have access to all the vital resources they need to build those advanced military units.

Industrialization

Industrialization ushers in the era of pollution. Starting with the Coal Plant and the Factory, this line of research leads to a whole string of city improvements that pollute. The lure of increased shield production makes Industrialization a popular advance for all strategies—just be prepared to deal with the pollution consequences.

NOTE

Industrialization also allows you to build the Universal Suffrage Wonder—a real bonus if you're governing by Republic or Democracy and a war might lie in your future.

Mass Production

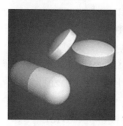

Mass Production is the Magnetism of the Industrial Ages. It is the single largest provider of modern naval power in the game. Plus, Mass Production is also the prerequisite for the mighty ground units provided by Amphibious War and (better still) Motorized Transportation. That said, this advance should take a back seat to more important advances such as Electronics and Flight unless you have an immediate need for naval units.

Medicine

Medicine is your best second choice for Industrial Age research after Nationalism. Medicine doesn't provide any immediate benefits, but it's a means to an end. Sanitation, the next advance in line, allows you to build Hospitals, which you need to allow your cities to grow past size 12.

You'll spend considerable time with zero population growth if you follow another line of research before Medicine.

Motorized Transportation

Tanks—you've gotta love 'em. If you're out to conquer the world, this unit really gets your efforts rolling—especially if you research Motorized Transportation well before your enemies do. The faster you get to Motorized Transportation, the more of an advantage you have in the ground war. Few things should sway you from your quest for Tanks (or Panzers, if you're playing the Germans) if conflict is your goal.

Nationalism

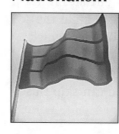

Just as Feudalism is a wise first choice for research when you reach the Middle Ages, Nationalism is your best bet when you hit the Industrial Ages. The reasoning is the same: No matter what strategy you prefer, good defensive units are of vital importance. Nationalism gives you Riflemen, which are significantly more efficient than Musketmen at keeping your cities safe.

Nationalism has a couple of hidden advantages as well. With Nationalism, you can sign mutual protection and trade embargo treaties. (For more info on these diplomatic options, see chapter V.) Better still, this advance allows you to obtain "free" military units by drafting your citizens into service.

TIP

If all you want is a defensive unit and there is no immediate threat to your security, skip Nationalism and make a run for Replaceable Parts (through Steam Power and Electricity). The Infantry unit allowed by that advance is twice as good as the Rifleman.

Radio

Radio is a late-Industrial Ages steppingstone advance. It provides you with no units, improvements, or Wonders. Its sole purpose is to allow you to research Advanced Flight. While this can be a very important advance if you're playing a military game, Radio serves little immediate advantage if Advanced Flight isn't part of your strategy. If you're not interested in Advanced Flight, you still have to research Radio to advance to Modern Times, but you can put if off for quite a while.

Refining

Refining is one of three advances that pave the way for Combustion. Like The Corporation and Steel, this advance offers no new units, improvements, or Wonders. One thing it *does* do, however, is reveal the Oil strategic resource on the map. For this reason, Refining should take precedence over Steel after you finish researching The Corporation. That way, you have time to access the newly found oil resources you need to build the modern naval units that are just around the corner.

Replaceable Parts

Replaceable Parts gives you a *huge* defensive upgrade in the form of the Infantry unit. Added bonuses include the Artillery unit, which greatly improves your bombardment capabilities (if you're into that sort of thing), and the appearance of the Rubber strategic resource. Most importantly, however, Replaceable Parts is one of the immediate prerequisites for Mass Production and all of the military might represented by it and its ensuing advances.

NOTE

An excellent side effect of researching Replaceable Parts is that it doubles the speed of your Workers.

Sanitation

 Sanitation looks like a dead-end advance— and, research-wise, it is. However, don't skip it. In fact, it should be high on your priority list when you enter the Industrial Ages. The reason is simple: Hospitals. Your cities can't grow beyond size 12, and thus can't reach their maximum potential without them.

NOTE

Sanitation also indirectly allows you to build the Battlefield Medicine Small Wonder, the prerequisite of which is to build five Hospitals. This gives Sanitation added importance when you're trying to conquer the world.

Scientific Method

 Scientific Method is an important step toward the pivotal Electronics advance. Unlike many of the second- and third-tier advances in the Industrial Ages, Scientific Method is more than just a link in the chain. It allows you to build the Theory of Evolution Wonder. Get to this advance as quickly as possible and be the first to build the Wonder. If you do, you get two free advances. It's a great way to speed your research efforts.

Steam Power

 Steam Power is a cornerstone advance of the Industrial Ages. It opens the door for just about every research topic available, and as such appears to be the most important advance to research at the start of the era. It's not. Despite its immediate and long-term advantages, both Nationalism and the Medicine/Sanitation combo should take precedence in most cases. (See the descriptions of those advances for the reasons.)

In addition to making the Ironclad unit possible, Steam Power allows your Workers to construct railroads and makes the Coal strategic resource appear.

Steel

Steel is a pivotal Industrial Age advance that (eventually) leads to the powerful mechanized and naval units that become available late in this era. Like The Corporation, Steel offers no immediate benefits. It is simply a means to a military end.

The Advances of Modern Times

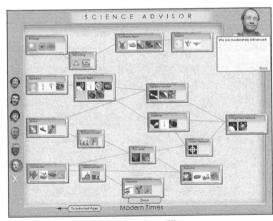

The research tree for Modern Times

Now you're in the research home stretch. The advances of Modern Times represent the pinnacle of human achievement. These ultra-scientific advances contribute to the betterment of your civilization and the world as a whole. Of course, that all depends on your ultimate goal. Some of

these advances also allow you to build very powerful weapons that can swiftly bring your opponents to their knees.

Computers

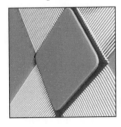

Of the four advances with which you can begin your Modern Times research, Computers offers the most useful and diverse immediate benefits. The Research Lab and the SETI Project give you a final science boost to get you through the expensive research times ahead, and the Mech Infantry unit provides the protection your cities need to weather military incursions spearheaded by the powerful ground units of this era. No matter what strategy you're following, there's no better advance with which to kick off Modern Times.

Ecology

Ecology is the beginning of a short but lucrative research path with something for everyone. The immediate benefits of Ecology are two pollution solutions: Solar Plants and Mass Transit. (See chapter IV for more info on pollution.) This isolated branch of the Modern research tree leads to additional pollution fixes (Recycling), spaceship parts, the most powerful ground

unit available (Synthetic Fibers), and, ultimately, the best air units this side of nukes (Stealth). Although Computers usually take precedence over Ecology, this advance should be a close second on your Modern Times "to do" list.

Fission

 Of the four initial Modern Times advances, Fission is the least desirable in most cases. Its immediate "benefits" (besides revealing the Uranium strategic resource) are only beneficial to the most warlike strategy. The Manhattan Project lets everyone build nukes (eventually), and Nuclear Subs helps you to deliver said nukes in a stealthy manner.

You ultimately need this advance to build your spaceship (if you're building one). But, unless nuclear warfare is your goal, pursue other available research paths first.

Genetics

 Genetics is a very specialized advance that, in most cases, can stay on the back burner for a long time. In fact, you could certainly win the game in a number of ways without every having access to the two Wonders that Genetics allows.

However, if you're pursuing a Cultural or Histographic Victory, don't let this advance slide altogether. The effects of the two Wonders combined (should you manage to build both of them) increase your population and help to create more happy people, and the Wonders themselves make a sizable contribution to your Culture Point total. If this is your goal, research Genetics as soon as possible so you can reap the maximum benefit from the two Wonders.

TIP

Building Wonders of the World increases your Culture Point total, whether you directly benefit from the Wonders or not. So, if you have the extra time and resources to build a Wonder such as the United Nations, do so. Even if you have no hope of winning a Diplomatic Victory, the Culture generated by the UN is still useful.

Integrated Defense

Civilization III, unlike its predecessor, doesn't have a city improvement that protects you against nuclear attacks. This job is now handled by the Strategic Missile Defense Small Wonder—and that's what Integrated Defense is all about.

This is one of those advances whose importance is determined solely by the current game situation. If you are up against enemies who are using nukes against you (or are threatening to do so), make a beeline for Integrated Defense. (The problem is, you have to research the bulk of the Modern advances to get here.) If no threat exists, ignore Integrated Defense until no other research options remain.

The Laser

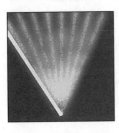

The Laser is a link in the chain that leads to Integrated Defense (through Smart Weapons) and Robotics. It is also a required Space Victory advance (you need The Laser to build the SS Planetary Party Lounge—you can't have a Planetary Party Lounge without a laser light show). Because it's a required advance no matter your strategy, you must research The Laser eventually. In terms of priority, it's usually

a toss-up between this advance and Superconductor. If you need Research Labs, research The Laser first.

Miniaturization

Miniaturization provides you with an opportunity to bump up shield output in your coastal cities—the Offshore Platform. However, this improvement is less important than the fact that Miniaturization is the prerequisite for Genetics (Cure for Cancer, Longevity) and Robotics (AEGIS Cruiser, Radar Artillery, and the Manufacturing Plant). At this stage in the game, most advances are about equally important, but give Miniaturization a lower priority than spaceship-oriented advances if you're heading for Alpha Centauri.

Nuclear Power

Nuclear Power is a positive benefit of Fission in that it gives you a clean way to boost your shield output—the Nuclear Plant. This advance is also a gateway to the benefits provided by Lasers and Robotics, and serves as a link in the spaceship chain as well.

There's no need research Nuclear Power immediately. If you need a clean power plant, research Ecology (the Solar Plant is safer and can be built in any city). This advance can wait until you've exhausted some of the other lines of research.

Recycling

Recycling shares equal importance with Ecology if you're experiencing pollution problems. Ecology's Mass Transit and Recycling's Recycling Center are a potent one-two punch that greatly reduces the possibility of pollution around your cities. If pollution is plaguing you, Recycling should be high on your list of Modern Times advances.

Robotics

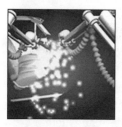

Robotics is an end-of-the-line advance that provides two military benefits (AEGIS Cruisers and Radar Artillery) and one universal benefit (Research Labs). Strive for this advance regardless of your strategy. If you're after the Research Labs, make a run for Robotics early in Modern Times—otherwise, the extra science will be of limited use.

Rocketry

Rocketry is immediately beneficial if you're on the road to conquest. Both the Jet Fighter (the F-15 for the Americans) and the Cruise Missile are valuable additions to your air-superiority arsenal. For the science-minded, Rocketry is one of the gateway advances to the Space Victory. Plus, Rocketry reveals Aluminum, one of the last hidden strategic resources.

Despite its benefits, Rocketry comes in a solid third out of the initial four Modern advances. Regardless of your strategy, get at least Ecology and Computers before you move on to this advance.

TIP

Rocketry might take precedence over Computers if your enemies are pummeling you with air units. In that case, the SAM Missile Battery provided by this advance is more important defensively than the Mech Infantry unit made available by Computers.

Satellites

In the wrong hands, this advance is potentially the game's most dangerous. Sure, the Satellites advance provides a spaceship component, which makes it a necessary advance for pacifists, but it also allows you to build ICBMs, the most deadly weapons in the game. Obviously, there's no avoiding this advance. Just remember, ICBMs cause more political and environmental trouble than you might be ready to deal with. Wise players ignore ICBMs even when they're available.

Smart Weapons

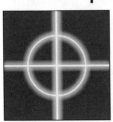

Besides being one of the final links in the Integrated Defense chain, Smart Weapons provides you with only one benefit—the ability to launch precision strike missions with your Stealth Fighters and Bombers. Obviously, this is only advantageous to you if you're waging war on your opponents *and* if you're using Stealth Fighters to do so. If both are true, Smart Weapons is a must-have advance. It is also important if you need to reach Integrated Defense and stave off nuclear attacks. Otherwise, put it off in favor of just about any other advance.

Space Flight

Space Flight is where the Space Victory begins to gather momentum. First, there's the Apollo Program Small Wonder, without which the journey to Alpha Centauri cannot begin. Three of the 10 spaceship components are also made possible by this advance. As a military footnote, Space Flight also gives you the ability to build Tactical Nukes (after you discover Fission and someone builds The Manhattan Project, that is). Space Flight is a natural extension of Rocketry, and should directly follow that advance in most research strategies.

Stealth

Stealth is one of the final Modern advances, and it is purely military in nature. For warrior-types, Stealth Bombers and Stealth Fighters can be integral to your strategy. However, if you're going for a nonconfrontational victory, either leave this advance until dead last or, better still, divert your science-dedicated commerce into luxuries and taxes to enhance the productivity of your empire and give you some extra cash to buy the spaceship pieces and/or defensive units you need to make it to the end of the game.

Superconductor

This advance is where Fission and Space Flight meet. Superconductor provides you with two more spaceship modules, so it's a vital technology for achieving the Space Victory. Don't ignore this advance if you are pursuing a military strategy, though. It's one of the prerequisites for Integrated Defense—an advance you'll need if you've ticked off your opponents enough that they're using nuclear weapons against you.

Synthetic Fibers

Like Rocketry, the primary benefits of Synthetic Fibers research are spaceship-related. This advance allows you to start building three of the 10 parts you need for your vessel (assuming the required strategic resources are available). As a bonus, Synthetic Fibers lets you build the ultimate ground attack unit—Modern Armor. If war is your chosen path to victory, this unit should seal your opponents' fate.

TIP

Always *research Rocketry before you research Synthetic Fibers. The Aluminum you need to build the spaceship parts and Modern Armor allowed by Synthetic Fibers is unavailable until after you discover Rocketry.*

Future Technology

Just because you've researched every advance listed on the research tree, that doesn't mean that scientific advancement grinds to a halt! After all of the named advances are discovered, you can continue your research with an endless string of Future Technologies. Future Technologies don't benefit you in any way *except* that each one adds to your Civilization Score.

If you're not playing the game for score, you can finally divert your commerce from science to taxes. This is just what you need to help you buy units to finish off your enemies or hurry the production of spaceship components so that you can be the first to reach Alpha Centauri.

RESEARCH STRATEGIES

Choosing research advances throughout the game is a dynamic process. Although you can follow certain guidelines based on your ultimate goal, many of the choices you make are based on what you need most when the choice must be made.

Because research is broken down into four ages in *Civ III*, your lines of research tend to be compartmentalized as well. That means that long-term research goals never extend beyond the end of the current age.

In the rest of this chapter, we'll take a look at the recommended research paths for both peaceful and warlike strategies in every age.

NOTE

The research paths described in this chapter are the recommended course of action under optimal conditions. Game conditions and the immediate needs of your empire often take precedence over your ultimate research goals. Don't hesitate to deviate from the recommended research track if you need a unit or improvement that is made possible by some other available advance.

Peace and Culture Research Paths

There are basically two ways to play *Civilization III*—peaceful coexistence and all-out military conflict. The peaceful method is, arguably, the more difficult path because it requires you to keep your opponents happy at all times. This isn't easy and, if you fail, the science-oriented research track you are pursuing can leave you without enough units to mount an effective counterattack when war breaks out.

The research paths for peaceful play emphasize resource production (with an emphasis on science and Culture) and overall empire growth, while providing for empire defense through the use of strong defensive units. This research pattern is mostly geared toward the Space Victory, but works equally well for Diplomatic, Cultural, and Histographic Victories.

NOTE

As discussed in chapter II, you should choose the civilization you control based on the type of victory you're trying to achieve. For the peaceful victory research path, we'll look at things from the Egyptian point of view. The Egyptians start the game with two advances: Ceremonial Burial and Masonry.

Ancient Times

The primary goal in Ancient Times is a better form of government. Of the two available in this era, The Republic is the better choice. No matter what deviations you have to make, keep this goal in sight at all times. The suggested research sequence is as follows:

1. Bronze Working
2. Alphabet
3. Writing
4. Literature
5. Mysticism
6. Pottery
7. Code of Laws
8. Philosophy
9. The Republic
10. Iron Working
11. Mathematics
12. Construction
13. Currency
14. The Wheel
15. Warrior Code
16. Horseback Riding
17. Polytheism
18. Monarchy
19. Map Making

Middle Ages

As is always true on the peaceful track, the first goal is to improve your defensive units. Afterward, Democracy is the goal in the Middle Ages, though there's a lot more crossover for useful defense-oriented military advances in this era.

1. Feudalism
2. Monotheism
3. Chivalry
4. Theology
5. Engineering
6. Invention
7. Gunpowder
8. Education
9. Astronomy
10. Music Theory
11. Printing Press
12. Democracy
13. Free Artistry
14. Banking
15. Economics
16. Chemistry
17. Navigation
18. Physics
19. Theory of Gravity
20. Metallurgy
21. Magnetism
22. Military Tradition (Optional)

Industrial Ages

The Industrial Ages starts off with a quest for defense and city growth. From there, it's mostly scientific advances, leaving most of the military advances for last.

1. Nationalism
2. Medicine
3. Sanitation
4. Steam Power
5. Electricity
6. Scientific Method
7. Replaceable Parts
8. Industrialization
9. Atomic Theory
10. Electronics
11. The Corporation
12. Refining
13. Steel
14. Combustion
15. Flight
16. Mass Production
17. Motorized Transportation
18. Radio
19. Advanced Flight (Optional)
20. Espionage (Optional)
21. Communism
22. Amphibious War (Optional)

Modern Times

In Modern Times, it's all about building your spaceship. Although it can be helpful to get Research Labs early, it's a bit of a hassle to get to Robotics quickly enough to make it matter much. So, concentrate on the advances that let you start building your spaceship as quickly as possible.

TIP

To increase your chances of winning a Cultural Victory, you might want to move Miniaturization and Genetics higher on the list so that you can get Cure for Cancer and Longevity earlier in the game.

1. Computers
2. Ecology
3. Recycling
4. Rocketry
5. Space Flight
6. Synthetic Fibers
7. Fission
8. Superconductor
9. Satellites
10. Nuclear Power
11. The Laser
12. Miniaturization
13. Genetics
14. Robotics
15. Stealth
16. Smart Weapons
17. Integrated Defense

Warmonger Research Paths

When you're trying to win by force, the best defense is a strong offense. If you're going for a Conquest or Domination Victory, you need to strike early and often while remaining ahead of your opponents' science curve to ensure that your units are better than theirs.

NOTE

For the exploration of the Conquest/Domination research paths, we'll look at things from the Japanese perspective. The Japanese start the game with Warrior Code and Ceremonial Burial.

Ancient Times

The first priority in the game is defense—never take an aggressive stance until you can defend yourself from retaliatory strikes. From there, your priorities are split between fast exploration, strong offensive units, and a better form of government. (Monarchy is the best choice for a warlike civilization in Ancient Times.)

TIP

If you think you can handle the war weariness problem, make a run for The Republic instead of Monarchy. While governing under a Republic makes war more difficult, it makes research and expansion a lot easier.

1. Bronze Working
2. Iron Working
3. Masonry
4. Alphabet
5. Mathematics
6. Construction
7. The Wheel
8. Horseback Riding
9. Mysticism
10. Polytheism
11. Monarchy
12. Writing
13. Literature
14. Pottery
15. Map Making
16. Code of Laws
17. Currency
18. Philosophy
19. The Republic (Optional)

Middle Ages

In the Middle Ages, military might becomes truly formidable. Start with a good defense (as always), then proceed along the offensive route. Because your empire is growing rapidly, you must occasionally step away from the warpath to research the advances that provide you with happiness-inducing improvements and Wonders.

1. Feudalism
2. Monotheism
3. Chivalry
4. Engineering
5. Invention
6. Gunpowder
7. Theology
8. Education
9. Astronomy
10. Chemistry
11. Metallurgy
12. Military Tradition
13. Physics
14. Magnetism
15. Theory of Gravity
16. Navigation
17. Banking
18. Music Theory
19. Economics
20. Printing Press (Optional)
21. Democracy (Optional)
22. Free Artistry (Optional)

Industrial Ages

In the Industrial Ages, you must first discover Communism. After this short quest, it's an all-out run for increased growth, shield production, and the powerful military units at the end of the era.

TIP

If you like to use subversive tactics rather than overt warfare, move Espionage higher on the list. The earlier you research this advance, the earlier you can begin your covert actions against the enemy.

1. Nationalism
2. Communism
3. Medicine
4. Sanitation
5. Steam Power
6. Industrialization
7. The Corporation
8. Refining
9. Steel
10. Combustion
11. Electricity
12. Replaceable Parts
13. Flight
14. Mass Production
15. Scientific Method
16. Atomic Theory
17. Electronics
18. Motorized Transportation
19. Amphibious Warfare
20. Radio
21. Advanced Flight
22. Espionage (Optional)

Modern Times

This is where the peaceful and aggressive strategies are most divergent. When conquest is your goal, you aren't looking for spaceship parts—you're looking for state-of-the-art weaponry! Now is the time to crush whatever enemies you have left.

1. Computers
2. Rocketry
3. Ecology
4. Recycling
5. Synthetic Fibers
6. Stealth
7. Fission
8. Space Flight
9. Satellites
10. Nuclear Power
11. The Laser
12. Smart Weapons
13. Miniaturization
14. Robotics
15. Superconductor
16. Integrated Defense
17. Genetics

VII

CITY IMPROVEMENTS AND WONDERS OF THE WORLD

Developing your cities is an ongoing process, and the decisions you make affect not only the population of each individual city, but the state of your empire as well. This has been true in every *Civilization*® game but, with the introduction of Culture Points and the new trade system (both of which are discussed in chapter V), every improvement and Wonder has a huge potential impact on the growth and prosperity of your civilization.

Every improvement and Wonder contributes to some aspect of your ongoing efforts—more shields, more Gold, happier citizens, or enhanced military might. Every time you're given the choice of what to build next, you must decide what benefits you

need most in the current situation. You cannot properly make this decision until you understand the benefits provided by each. That's what this chapter is all about.

CITY IMPROVEMENTS

Every city improvement, big or small, adds to the infrastructure of your cities. In the *Civilization III* game, with the addition of Culture and the new system of trade, the improvements provide an even more diverse array of benefits, both to the city where they're constructed and your empire at large.

Table 7-1 lists all of the city improvements and their vital statistics. The statistics listed for each are:

- **Cost:** The number of shields it costs to build the improvement.

- **Maintenance:** The amount of Gold subtracted from your treasury each turn to maintain the improvement.

- **Culture:** The number of Culture Points generated by the improvement per turn.

- **Prerequisites:** The advance that you must discover, the improvement you must build, and/or the strategic resource to which you must have access before you can build the improvement.

- **Effects:** The function served by the improvement.

TABLE 7-1. IMPROVEMENT STATISTICS

IMPROVEMENT	COST	MAINTENANCE	CULTURE	PREREQUISITES	EFFECTS
Airport	160	2	—	Flight	City produces veteran air units; trade link to other cities with Airports; allows airlifts.
Aqueduct	100	1	—	Construction	City can grow beyond population 6.
Bank	120	2	—	Banking; Marketplace	City tax revenue increases by 50% (cumulative with Marketplace).
Barracks	40	1	—	—	City produces veteran ground units.
Cathedral	140	2	3	Monotheism	Makes 3 unhappy citizens in the city content.
Coal Plant	160	3	—	Industrialization; Factory; Coal	Factory output increases by 50%
Coastal Fortress	60	2	—	Metallurgy; Iron; Saltpeter	City has a naval bombardment defense of 8 and 50% defensive bonus vs. naval attacks; automatically bombards passing enemy ships.
Colosseum	120	2	2	Construction	Makes 2 unhappy citizens in the city content.
Courthouse	80	1	—	Code of Laws	Corruption in the city decreases and the effects of propaganda lessen.
Factory	200	3	—	Industrialization; Iron	City's shield production increases by 50%
Granary	60	1	—	Pottery	Only half the city's food is depleted when the population grows.
Harbor	80	1	—	Map Making	City produces veteran naval units; coastal, sea, and ocean squares produce +1 food; trade link to other cities with Harbors.

continued on next page

TABLE 7-1. IMPROVEMENT STATISTICS, CONTINUED

IMPROVEMENT	COST	MAINTENANCE	CULTURE	PREREQUISITES	EFFECTS
Hospital	120	2	—	Sanitation	City can grow beyond size 12.
Hydro Plant	240	3	—	Electronics; Factory; river in city radius	Factory output increases by 50%
Library	80	1	3	Literature	City's science output increases by 50%
Manufacturing Plant	320	3	—	Robotics; Factory	City's shield production increases by 50% (cumulative with Factory).
Marketplace	80	1	—	Currency	City's tax revenue increases by 50%; the number of happy faces produced by luxuries increases.
Mass Transit System	160	2	—	Ecology; Rubber	Pollution caused by city's population is reduced.
Nuclear Plant	160	3	—	Nuclear Power; Factory; Uranium; water inside the city radius	Factory output increases by 50%
Offshore Platform	160	3	—	Miniaturization	All Coast, Sea, and Ocean squares in the city radius produce 1 shield.
Palace	100	—	1	Masonry	Corruption and waste in the capital is eliminated and both decrease in nearby cities.
Police Station	80	2	—	Communism	The effects of war weariness in the city are lessened.
Recycling Center	200	2	—	Recycling	Pollution caused by the city's improvements decreases.
Research Lab	160	2	2	Computers; University	City's science output increases by 50% (cumulative with Library and University).
SAM Missile Battery	80	2	—	Rocketry; Aluminum	Enemy air units attacking the city are fired on.
Solar Plant	320	3	—	Ecology; Factory	Factory increases output by 50%
SS Cockpit	160	0	—	Space Flight; Aluminum	Necessary component for the Alpha Centauri Spaceship.

continued on next page

TABLE 7-1. IMPROVEMENT STATISTICS, CONTINUED

IMPROVEMENT	COST	MAINTENANCE	CULTURE	PREREQUISITES	EFFECTS
SS Docking Bay	160	0	—	Space Flight; Aluminum	Necessary component for the Alpha Centauri Spaceship.
SS Engine	320	0	—	Space Flight; Aluminum	Necessary component for the Alpha Centauri Spaceship.
SS Exterior Casing	320	0	—	Synthetic Fibers; Aluminum; Rubber	Necessary component for the Alpha Centauri Spaceship.
SS Fuel Cells	160	0	—	Superconductor; Uranium	Necessary component for the Alpha Centauri Spaceship.
SS Life Support System	320	0	—	Superconductor; Aluminum	Necessary component for the Alpha Centauri Spaceship.
SS Planetary Party Lounge	160	0	—	The Laser; Aluminum	Necessary component for the Alpha Centauri Spaceship.
SS Stasis Chamber	320	0	—	Synthetic Fibers; Aluminum	Necessary component for the Alpha Centauri Spaceship.
SS Storage/Supply	160	0	—	Synthetic Fibers; Aluminum	Necessary component for the Alpha Centauri Spaceship.
SS Thrusters	160	0	—	Satellites; Aluminum	Necessary component for the Alpha Centauri Spaceship.
Temple	40	1	2	Ceremonial Burial	One unhappy citizen in the city becomes content.
University	160	2	4	Education; Library	City's science output increases by 50% (cumulative with Library).
Walls	20	0	—	Masonry	City has a land bombardment defense of 8; garrisoned units in the city receive a 50% defensive bonus.
Wealth	0	0	—	—	The city's shields convert into Gold at a ratio of 8:1 (4:1 after the discovery of Economics).

In practice, most large cities build every available improvement by the end of the game. To be an effective leader, you need to know when to build improvements so that your empire reaps the maximum benefit from each—without going broke in the process. The descriptions in the following sections analyze the pros and cons of each improvement.

Airport

The new trade system in *Civilization III* has greatly increased the importance of Airports. As important as the air combat and airlift by this improvement is the trade link it provides. Any city in your empire with an Airport trades strategic resources with all of your other Airport-equipped cities. If vast distances separate your cities, Airports are the most reliable way to provide your distant cities with vital resources they might not otherwise have access to. Make sure that any city that has access to a vital strategic resource is equipped with this improvement.

Aqueduct

Veteran players will remember that Aqueducts used to be "must have" improvements in every city—without this improvement, a city couldn't grow beyond a certain point. This is still true to some extent, although any city with fresh water inside its radius (rivers or inland seas) doesn't require Aqueducts to grow.

> **TIP**
>
> *Wait until your city reaches size 4 or 5 before you construct this improvement. Don't waste precious Gold maintaining the Aqueduct before you need it.*

Bank

When the cost of maintaining your improvements and supporting your units becomes too great, your Marketplaces can't keep up with the tax burden. Banks ease your monetary woes without the need to create tax collectors. If you build Banks in at least five of your cities, you can construct the Wall Street Small Wonder, which does even more to increase your cash reserves. While

happiness-inducing improvements must usually take precedence, don't wait too long before you start saving for the future.

Barracks

 The benefits of building Barracks early the game are obvious, especially if you're out to eliminate your neighbors. The veteran ground units produced by Barracks also benefit you throughout the game. Don't build too many Barracks too early, though, or you risk depleting your treasury with too many maintenance fees.

When you have five cities with Barracks, you can build the Military Academy Small Wonder—an important addition to any conquer-the-world strategy.

NOTE

Civ® II veterans will be happy to know that Barracks no longer expire as your technology advances. One Barracks now lasts the entire game.

Cathedral

 The importance of Cathedrals can't be overstated—the higher the game difficulty level, the more important they are. Cathedrals are one of the best ways to keep your people happy, plus they provide a significant Culture boost.

TIP

If you build the Sistine Chapel Wonder, you can save on maintenance costs by not building Cathedrals in the cities on the same continent as the Wonder. However, if you can afford it, building multiple Cathedrals in addition to the Wonder provides more Culture Points.

Coal Plant

 The Coal Plant is the equivalent of the Power Plant in *Civilization II*. This is the first power plant you can build, and the shield boost it provides is very tempting. But, before you start building Coal Plants in all of your cities, consider the pollution consequences. Unless you desperately need the extra shields, wait

until you discover Electronics and can build Hydro Plants instead (in the cities where you can do so). If you *do* build Coal Plants, replace them with cleaner power plants as they become available.

> **NOTE**
>
> Only one type of power plant can operate in each city. Building a power plant in a city that already has one eliminates the effects of previous power plant.

Coastal Fortress

Coastal Fortresses are Walls to protect coastal cities from naval attacks—only better, because they don't go away when the city grows beyond Town size. Build this improvement based on the amount of ship traffic in the vicinity. If lots of enemy ships are about, play it safe and build a Coastal Fortress in every coastal town in the high-traffic areas. Otherwise, save the maintenance expenses.

Colosseum

Colosseums are always useful in keeping your population content but, like all other "happiness" improvements and Wonders, their importance increases with game difficulty. This improvement offers an excellent interim solution to unhappiness problems caused by rapid city and empire growth during Ancient Times—the perfect stopgap measure when Temples aren't enough and Cathedrals aren't yet available. As an added bonus, they increase your Culture Points as well.

> **NOTE**
>
> Colosseums no longer increase in effectiveness after the discovery of Electronics. Their benefit remains static throughout the game.

Courthouse

If you like to spread your empire far and wide early in the game, integrate Courthouses into your strategy. They stem the loss of shields and Gold to waste and corruption, and every little bit helps.

Without them, cities far from your capital suffer from sluggish production and contribute little in the way of commerce.

> **NOTE**
>
> Courthouses no longer make one citizen happy under a Democracy.

> **TIP**
>
> *You can slow the rate of corruption and waste with improvements and Wonders, but the long-term solution to these problems is your system of government. The more advanced your government is, the less trouble you'll have with corruption and waste.*

Factory

 Factories are both a blessing and a curse. The cost of improvements, Wonders, and units increases as time goes on, and by the beginning of the Industrial Ages you can use a good shield boost. Unfortunately, this comes at the expense of pollution risks.

Always build a Factory in any city whose shield production is substandard. In other cities, balance your desire for fast production with your ability to deal with pollution. Remember: no pollution-cutting improvements are available this early in the game.

Granary

 To build a Granary or not is hotly debated among *Civ* veterans discussing early-game strategies. The rapid city growth provided by this improvement is a great boon to production and empire growth. Unfortunately, in a fertile environment your growth can easily outpace your ability to keep your population happy. This is especially true on the higher difficulty levels.

When playing at King level or higher, delay building Granaries until after you discover Ceremonial Burial, which allows you to counteract unhappiness by building Temples. Regardless of difficulty level, don't rush to build Granaries in cities that are already growing steadily.

> **TIP**
>
> *Remember, building The Pyramids gives you the Granary benefit in all of your cities on the same continent as the Wonder. If you can't deal with the potential unhappiness problems, delay building The Pyramids.*

Harbor

Harbors are cheap to build and cheap to maintain—which is awesome, considering their benefits and strategic importance. Harbors increase the food benefits you get from the neighboring Coast, Sea, and Ocean terrain, and allow the city to produce veteran sea units. In addition, Harbors now connect you to the all-important trade network. Your Harbor-equipped cities can trade strategic resources back and forth, giving your distant cities access to vital resources that might otherwise be unavailable to them. Equip all of your coastal cities with Harbors.

TIP

Harbors are less effective than Airports for distant trade routes. Trade between two Harbor cities requires a clear water route between them, with no intervening unexplored squares or enemy units blocking the invisible path. Because of this, naval blockades can be created to choke overseas trade to a city. All the enemy has to do is occupy every Coast, Sea, or Ocean square that touches the city square itself. Use this trick to cut off your enemies' internal overseas trade routes—and be careful lest they do the same to you.

Hospital

At first glance, this seems to be a new improvement. However, savvy veteran players will recognize its effects as being the same as those of the Sewer System in *Civilization II*.

This is truly a "must have" improvement. Without a Hospital, a city can't grow beyond size 12. As with Aqueducts, there's no need to build a Hospital right away. Wait until a city reaches size 10 or so before you start building this improvement. However, if you're embroiled in a war and have lots of units in enemy territory (or expect to in the near future), add a Hospital to at least five of your cities so that you can construct the Battlefield Medicine Small Wonder, which allows your troops to heal while outside your empire's borders.

Hydro Plant

The Hydro Plant is the second of the two Industrial Age power plants. It's worth waiting for in most cases, and much preferable to Coal Plants, since Hydro Plants produce no pollution. The catch is that Hydro Plants can only be built in cities that have a river within their radius. For these cities, the choice of power plants is a no-brainer.

> **NOTE**
>
> Hydro, Nuclear, and Solar Plants in
> *Civ III* no longer provide the pollution-
> reduction bonuses they provided in
> *Civ II*. They merely don't *add* to the
> pollution problem like a Coal Plant does.

Library

One of the surest paths to defeat is to fall behind your opponents in the technology race. The faster you research advances, the sooner you gain a technological advantage. That translates into a military advantage in the form of better units.

The Library is the first of three improvements that boost a city's science output. Unless you have other problems (unhappiness, for instance) build a Library in every city after you discover Literature. The additional Culture Points you receive are an added bonus.

Manufacturing Plant

Before a city can build this improvement, it must already have a Factory. The two improvements work together to double the city's shield output.

Increased shield output can be useful, but

this improvement comes with the same caveat as does the Factory—be prepared to deal with the pollution consequences. Cities with both a Factory and a Manufacturing Plant should never be saddled with a "dirty" Coal Plant. If you need additional shields, choose a Hydro, Nuclear, or Solar Plant instead.

Marketplace

The Marketplace is often ignored until the treasury starts running low. That's a mistake, especially considering its new happiness effects. The Marketplace now stems unhappiness in the city where it's built based on the number of luxuries the city produces (see Table 7-2).

TABLE 7-2.
MARKETPLACE HAPPINESS EFFECTS

LUXURIES PRODUCED BY CITY	*NUMBER OF HAPPY FACES PRODUCED*
1st and 2nd	1
3rd and 4th	2
5th and 6th	3
7th and 8th	4

The new Marketplace keeps your people happy and increases tax revenue. For happiness purposes, this improvement obviously works best in cities with lots of luxuries.

Mass Transit System

Cities can pollute merely because they have a high population. That's where Mass Transit comes in. Late in the game, this improvement becomes a vital tool in the prevention of global warming. When you discover Ecology, make sure all of your cities have access to Rubber, and start building Mass Transit Systems in each city to ease your pollution woes.

NOTE

The Mass Transit System no longer prevents *all* population-produced pollution in a city as it did in *Civ II*—but it's still a very important and effective improvement.

Nuclear Plant

Nuclear Plants are more cost-effective than Hydro Plants and have the same benefit of producing no pollution. The drawback to this shield-boosting improvement is the possibility of a meltdown— a catastrophic pollution-propagating event that can occur when your government falls into Anarchy for any

reason. However, the chance of a meltdown is sufficiently slim (especially if you have a stable government and don't change governments often), making Nuclear Plants worth the risk.

NOTE

Veteran players should note that Nuclear Plants in *Civ III* can only be built in cities that have at least one water square (Coast, Sea, Ocean, River) inside the city radius.

Offshore Platform

The usefulness of an Offshore Platform depends on the number of Coast/Sea/Ocean squares within the city radius and the number of those

squares currently in use. In cities where few of these terrain squares are available or where the population is so small that few of them are being worked, the construction and upkeep costs can outweigh the improvement's benefits. Offshore Platforms can be put off indefinitely in favor of more beneficial improvements.

Palace

The Palace is the only improvement you receive automatically—it is built in your first city, thereby designating that as your capital. You can only have one Palace. If you build it in another city, it is eliminated from its current location when the new one is built.

In *Civilization III,* the zero corruption and zero waste benefits provided by the Palace can be duplicated in another city by building the Forbidden Palace Small Wonder.

Police Station

Although its method of operation has changed since *Civ II,* the function of the Police Station remains unchanged. This is an invaluable improvement late in the game, especially if you're pursuing a violent strategy under a Republic or a Democracy. The more Police Stations you have, the less impact extended military campaigns have on your population—that is, war weariness is greatly reduced.

Recycling Center

A Recycling Center works hand-in-hand with a Mass Transit System to greatly reduce a city's pollution output. In cities where the pollution risk is extremely high, don't put off this improvement or you risk global warming.

Research Lab

The Research Lab is the third jewel in the science improvement triple crown. When added to an existing Library and University, the city's science output is increased by a whopping 150 percent! It also increases the city's Culture Points. There's no excuse to not build a Research Lab in every city—especially if you plan to compete in the space race or achieve a Cultural Victory.

> **TIP**
>
> *To further enhance your science output, consider building science-inducing Wonders such as Copernicus's Observatory and the SETI Program.*

SAM Missile Battery

If you're up against an opponent who likes to attack from the air, build SAM missile batteries in all of your cities within bombing range of that enemy's border. Essentially, this improvement provides the same benefits against air units that the Coastal Fortress provides against naval units. Build them in any city that's in danger of air attack.

TIP

There's no SDI Defense improvement in Civ III, and the SAM Missile Battery provides no defense against nuclear attack. To protect yourself from nukes, build SAMs in at least five of your cities, and then build the Strategic Missile Defense Small Wonder.

Solar Plant

Solar Plants in *Civilization III* function identically to Nuclear Plants except for one significant advantage: no meltdowns. For the higher construction and upkeep costs, you get a clean power plant that is perfectly safe even if your government goes up in smoke.

Build Solar Plants only if you're a habitual government switcher or if you anticipate the frequent fall of your government due to civil unrest. They are also fine alternatives to Nuclear Plants in cities without access to water.

Spaceship (SS) Components

Civilization III boasts 10 different spaceship components (as opposed to five in the previous games), but the principle is the same—to achieve the Alpha Centauri victory, you must build some of each in specified numbers and combinations. If you're going for some other form of victory, you don't need them at all. So, it's not a matter of which component is more or less important—it's just a matter of how quickly you can build them.

The function of each component and the number and combinations needed to construct a viable spaceship are detailed in chapter IX.

NOTE

Familiarize yourself with the prerequisites for building spaceship components. It's not just a matter of having the right technology— strategic resources are involved, too.

Temple

This is the earliest happiness improvement in the game and should, arguably, be the first improvement you build in every city. This is especially true on the higher difficulty levels, where the restless population requires as much early appeasement as possible. Having Temples in place early allows your cities to grow more smoothly.

NOTE

Temples no longer increase in effectiveness after the discovery of Mysticism. Their benefit remains static throughout the game.

University

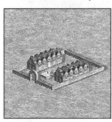

The second of the three big science improvements, the University combines with an existing Library to double a city's science output. At the stage in the game when this improvement becomes available, advances are starting to get expensive—it costs more science to discover them. Given this, every city should have a University.

Walls

Several things about Walls (formerly City Walls) have changed. While they're still well worth having— especially considering their zero maintenance cost—don't expect the same performance out of them. They now provide only a 50 percent defensive bonus (as opposed to 300 percent in *Civ II*), though this is offset somewhat by the bombardment bonus they provide.

Walls are the only improvements that expire. When your city grows beyond Town status (a population of 6), the beneficial effects of Walls are lost.

NOTE

Despite the bombardment defense they provide, Walls *can* be destroyed by bombardments.

Wealth

Civ II veterans will remember this improvement as Capitalization. The principle is the same, but there are a couple of changes, one of which is the exchange rate: 8 shields = 1 Gold before Economics; 4 shields = 1 Gold thereafter.

Despite being less profitable, Wealth is more useful because it's available from the beginning of the game. This is the perfect thing to "build" when no improvements or Wonders are available and you don't need any more units. It's also a great way to raise Gold when you need to hurry production or build up a support stockpile for an upcoming military action.

SMALL WONDERS AND WONDERS OF THE WORLD

You build Wonders just as you would city improvements. They're a lot more expensive than improvements, but their effects are more far-reaching and dramatic. Many Wonders produce the same effects as city improvements. The difference is that Wonder effects often benefit many (if not all) of your cities. Wonders of the World are exclusive—as soon as a Wonder is built, it becomes unavailable to all other civilizations.

Civilization III introduces the concept of Small Wonders—minor achievements and structures whose effects are less pronounced or widespread than normal Wonders of the World. Unlike Wonders of the World, Small Wonders can be built by every civilization in the game.

NOTE

Although many of the Wonders in *Civilization III* have the same names as their *Civ II* predecessors, many of their effects have been significantly altered. Even if you're a veteran player, take the time to read through this section. Some of your old strategies won't work anymore.

Table 7-3 lists all of the Wonders of the World and their vital statistics. The statistics listed for each are:

- **Cost:** The number of shields it costs to build the Wonder.

- **Culture:** The number of Culture Points generated by the Wonder per turn.

- **Prerequisite:** The advance, improvement, and/or strategic resource you must possess or the condition that must be met before you can build the Wonder.

- **Obsolete:** The advance that cancels the effects of the Wonder.

- **Effects:** The function served by the Wonder.

TABLE 7-3. WONDER STATISTICS

WONDER	COST	CULTURE	PREREQUISITE	OBSOLETE	EFFECTS
* Apollo Program	400	3	Space Flight; Aluminum	—	Enables you to begin construction of your Alpha Centauri Spaceship.
* Battlefield Medicine	380	1	5 Hospitals	—	Allows your units to heal in enemy territory.
The Colossus	220	3	Bronze Working	Flight	Generates one extra unit of commerce in any square already producing commerce in the city where it's built.
Copernicus's Observatory	420	4	Astronomy	—	Doubles scientific research in the city where it's built.
Cure for Cancer	800	5	Genetics	—	Makes one unhappy citizen content in all of your cities.
* Forbidden Palace	220	3	8 Cities	—	Provides the benefits of a Palace in the city where it's built.
The Great Library	300	5	Literature	Education	Automatically gives you any advance that has been discovered by at least two other civilizations.
The Great Lighthouse	200	2	Map Making	Magnetism	Allows Galleys to move safely in and out of sea squares; increases the movement of all naval units by one.
The Great Wall	240	2	Construction	Metallurgy	Doubles the effects of Walls in your cities that have them; doubles unit attack strength versus Barbarians.
The Hanging Gardens	260	4	Monarchy	Steam Power	Makes 3 unhappy citizens content in the city where it's built and 1 unhappy citizen content in all of your other cities.
* Heroic Epic	240	4	Army victory	—	Increases the appearance of Leaders from victorious combat.
Hoover Dam	540	3	Electronics	—	Acts as a Hydro Plant in all of your cities on the same continent.
* Intelligence Agency	300	1	Espionage	—	Enables you to undertake espionage missions.
* Iron Works	200	2	Coal and Iron in city radius	—	Increases production by 100% in the city where it's built.

continued on next page

TABLE 7-3. WONDER STATISTICS, CONTINUED

WONDER	COST	CULTURE	PREREQUISITE	OBSOLETE	EFFECTS
JS Bach's Cathedral	460	5	Music Theory	—	Decreases the number of unhappy citizens by 2 in every city on the same continent.
Leonardo's Workshop	520	2	Invention	—	Allows you to upgrade obsolete units at half the normal cost.
Longevity	700	3	Genetics	—	Population in all cities increase by 2 (instead of 1) when the food storage box is filled.
Magellan's Voyage	410	3	Navigation	—	Movement rate of all naval units is increased by 1.
The Manhattan Project	580	2	Fission; Uranium	—	Allows the construction of nuclear weapons by all civilizations.
* Military Academy	150	1	Military Tradition; 5 Barracks	—	Allows the construction of Armies without Leaders in the city where it's built.
Newton's University	500	5	Theory of Gravity	—	Doubles scientific research in the city where it's built.
The Oracle	260	4	Mysticism	Theology	Doubles the effects of all Temples in your empire.
* The Pentagon	180	1	3 Armies in the field	—	Increases the unit capacity of your Armies from 3 to 4.
The Pyramids	400	4	Masonry	—	Acts as a Granary in all of your cities on the same continent.
SETI Program	700	3	Computers	—	Doubles scientific research in the city where it's built.
Shakespeare's Theater	440	5	Free Artistry	—	Makes 8 unhappy citizens content in the city where it's built.
Sistine Chapel	540	4	Theology	—	Doubles the effect of all Cathedrals in your cities.
Smith's Trading Company	400	3	Economics	—	Pays maintenance costs for all Marketplaces, Banks, Harbors, and Airports.

continued on next page

TABLE 7-3. WONDER STATISTICS, CONTINUED

WONDER	COST	CULTURE	PREREQUISITE	OBSOLETE	EFFECTS
* Strategic Missile Defense	320	1	Integrated Defense; 5 SAM Missile Batteries	—	Has a 75% chance of intercepting enemy ICBMs.
Sun Tzu's Art of War	340	2	Feudalism	—	Provides all of the Barracks benefits to each of your cities on the continent where it is built.
Theory of Evolution	550	3	Scientific Method	—	Automatically grants 2 advances when completed.
The United Nations	600	4	Radio	—	Allows the possibility of achieving a Diplomatic Victory.
Universal Suffrage	580	4	Industrialization	—	Reduces war weariness in all of your cities.

* Denotes Small Wonders

TIP

Remember—Small Wonders are not exclusive like their grander counterparts. They can be built by every civilization in the game. When you have to make a choice between a Small Wonder and a Wonder of the World, build the Wonder of the World first so you can beat your opponents to the punch. You can always come back to the Small Wonders later.

Apollo Program (Small Wonder)

The Apollo Program is pivotal in that building it is the only way that you can achieve the Space Victory. You must have access to Aluminum to build this Wonder.

With its "demotion" to a Small Wonder, the tried-and-true *Civilization* tactic of waiting for an opponent to foot the cost of construction and reaping the benefits of their hard work is no longer a valid strategy. To join the space race, you must build the Apollo Program yourself.

If you plan to win via the space race, build this Wonder as soon as it becomes available so that you can beat your opponents to the punch. Otherwise, ignore it until you have production resources to spare.

NOTE
Veteran players should note that building the Apollo Program no longer reveals the entire world map.

Battlefield Medicine (Small Wonder)

This new Wonder is a vital component of any militaristic strategy. The ability for units to heal themselves outside of your sphere of influence allows you to press an advance far into enemy territory without having to backtrack with your wounded units. To build Battlefield Medicine, at least five of your cities must have Hospitals. Even if you don't follow a gung-ho military strategy, you can still reap the benefits of this Wonder in the minor skirmishes you're bound to encounter.

The Colossus

The Colossus provides an excellent early-game commerce and Culture boost. It's inexpensive as far as Wonders go, and its benefits can be significant if you build it in the right city. Build this Wonder in a city that produces a lot of commerce.

NOTE
You can build The Colossus only in cities that border Sea squares. (Inland seas don't count.) This is also true of The Great Lighthouse and Magellan's Voyage.

Copernicus's Observatory

Always take advantage of increases in science. Copernicus's Observatory's effects are cumulative with all science-enhancing improvements (Libraries, Universities, and so on). In fact, the effects of this Wonder are calculated *after* the effects of city improvements and scientists.

Depending on your situation, this Wonder might have to take a back seat to other Wonders such as JS Bach's Cathedral.

However, if you manage to build it, Copernicus's Observatory pays off handsomely in the long run.

> **TIP**
>
> *Want to generate a killer amount of science? Build Copernicus's Observatory in the same city as Newton's University.*

Cure for Cancer

 By the time this Wonder becomes available, your empire is probably governed by an advanced form of government such as a Republic or a Democracy. Under these systems the happiness of your citizens can be difficult to maintain.

This late-game Wonder acts as a permanent Entertainer in every one of your cities. If your luxuries are scarce or you're embroiled in a drawn-out conflict, Cure for Cancer is indispensable. It's one of the top-priority Wonders of Modern Times.

Forbidden Palace (Small Wonder)

 As your empire expands farther from your capital, waste and corruption increase. Advanced governments and city improvements such as Courthouses and Police Stations help, but these solutions aren't available early in the game.

The Forbidden Palace Wonder is an excellent way to patch the corruption and waste problem if your empire grows to eight cities or more very early in the game. Build it in the city experiencing the most corruption and waste to maximize the Wonder's effects.

The Great Library

 The Great Library is easily the most important Wonder of Ancient Times—especially if you find yourself way behind your opponents in research. Point your research toward Literature just so you can build The Great Library. Pick your most productive city and pull out all the stops to make sure that you, not one of your opponents, build this vital Wonder.

TIP

Pacifist players will find The Great Library especially useful when up against two or more militaristic opponents. While you're pursuing a peaceful line of research, the free advances you get courtesy of your warmongering neighbors' militaristic research allows you to keep your defensive forces up to date.

The Great Lighthouse

Whether or not The Great Lighthouse is a "must have" Wonder is based on your dependency on sea travel early in the game. If you're stuck on a small island and you need to expand overseas, this Wonder's benefits are obvious. However, these benefits are rather short-lived due to the Wonder's (usually) early expiration. The Culture boost is also minimal. As ancient Wonders go, this is usually a low-priority one.

NOTE

The Great Lighthouse no longer grants veteran status to all naval units built while it is active as it did in *Civilization II.*

The Great Wall

Of all of the ancient Wonders, The Great Wall has gone through the most changes since *Civilization II*. It no longer has any effect on rival civilizations with regard to peace treaties, and it now doubles the defensive value of existing Walls rather than acting as walls in all of your cities.

Considering these changes, the priority of this Wonder has been somewhat reduced. Build The Great Wall before the other ancient Wonders only if you are embroiled in an early-game war and need the extra defensive strength for your Walls.

TIP

Building Wonders early in the game is time consuming. Wait until you have several thriving cities before you commit one of them to producing a Wonder. That way, the other cities can produce vital units while the Wonder-city is occupied.

The Hanging Gardens

The importance of The Hanging Gardens increases with the game difficulty level. Unhappiness is rampant at the higher levels, so you need all the help you can get to keep your cities out of civil unrest. Even at the lower difficulty levels, this Wonder can ease the unhappiness that accompanies rapid empire growth. The high Culture bonus is merely icing on the cake. Along with The Great Library and The Oracle, make The Hanging Gardens a priority in Ancient Times.

Heroic Epic (Small Wonder)

For militaristic players, Armies are a big boon when it comes to wreaking havoc on the enemy. Unless you have a Military Academy, the only way to create an army is with a Leader—and Leaders are scarce.

Heroic Epic is definitely worth building, though not at the expense of more important ancient Wonders, such as The Great Library or The Hanging Gardens. Chances are slim that you'll have the opportunity anyway, because you must already have at least one victorious Army before this Wonder becomes available. Only warmongers need apply.

Hoover Dam

The Hoover Dam is an important Wonder in the Industrial Ages when increased shield production usually means copious amounts of pollution. The increase in shield production this Wonder provides comes without the burden of pollution, just like the Hydro Plant it emulates. Even if you don't have a shield shortage when this Wonder becomes available, make its construction a priority. It saves you the production time and maintenance cost of building individual Coal, Hydro, Nuclear, or Solar Plants in every city.

> **TIP**
>
> *Build the Hoover Dam Wonder on the continent that houses the bulk of your cities. Unlike the Hoover Dam in Civilization II, this version only affects cities on the continent where it is built.*

Intelligence Agency (Small Wonder)

Many *Civilization* veterans have formed strategies that heavily depend on spy-related activity. Because Diplomats and Spies don't exist in *Civ III*, the Intelligence Agency is a vital Wonder for those who depend on underhanded trickery to accomplish your goals.

Think carefully before you make the Intelligence Agency a top priority, however. Several very important Wonders in the Industrial Ages (Hoover Dam, Universal Suffrage, and Battlefield Medicine to name a few) have practical and Cultural benefits with a greater impact than those of the Intelligence Agency.

Iron Works (Small Wonder)

The strategic resource model in *Civilization III* provides an excellent opportunity to create a super-producing city very early in the game.

If you're lucky enough to find a potential city site that has both Coal and Iron within its city radius, build a city there. Once you do, you immediately have the opportunity to build the Iron Works—and you should!

The increased production you reap gives you a production center that can produce anything you want. In fact, such a city, with its large shield production, can make it possible to beat your opponents in the race for the early Wonders of the World.

> **TIP**
>
> *If the city where you build the Iron Works is distant from your capital, build the Forbidden Palace in the same city. The increased productivity of the city is worthless if you lose most of the additional shields to waste.*

JS Bach's Cathedral

This already-vital Wonder has gained even more importance with the addition of the Culture element of *Civ III*. When playing at the higher difficulty levels, or governing by Republic or Democracy, this Wonder's ability to dispel unhappiness is almost essential to your success. Having that extra buffer of two fewer unhappy people in the bulk of your cities makes growth and conducting military campaigns much easier in the later stages of the game.

TIP

Build JS Bach's Cathedral on the continent that contains most of your cities. Unlike the Civ II version, the effects are now confined to the continent where the Wonder is built.

Leonardo's Workshop

 Although it is still one of the more important Wonders of the Middle Ages, Leonardo's Workshop is not quite as powerful as it was in *Civilization II*.

Leonardo's Workshop now halves the cost of upgrading units. This Wonder no longer expires—which means the savings last throughout the game. The Gold this Wonder can save, especially when you're following a militaristic path, is substantial. In most cases, however, other Wonders of the era, such as JS Bach's Cathedral, should take priority.

Longevity

 Late in the game, fast city growth can be a real boon to your production efforts— whether you're building up your military to wipe out that final enemy or trying to complete your spaceship before your opponents do.

The doubled population growth provided by Longevity can cause major headaches if you don't properly plan for it. Develop improvements and Wonders to handle both pollution and unhappiness before Longevity comes on line. Otherwise, the rapidly growing population will have you scrambling to quell disorder and pollution all over your empire.

Magellan's Voyage

 Magellan's Voyage takes over where The Great Lighthouse leaves off, providing your naval units with additional movement. Like its ancient predecessor, the importance of this Wonder depends on whether your strategy or map position requires extensive ocean travel. If it does, the added advantage of the extra movement point can give you a tactical edge over your seagoing opponents. If naval travel and combat are low on your priority list, Magellan's Voyage should be as well.

The Manhattan Project

The Manhattan Project opens a deadly can of worms by giving *every* civilization the potential to produce nuclear weapons. Unless you need or desire to escalate a nuclear conflict, leave this Wonder to your opponents. The Culture gain is meager, and the potential dangers are great. Let your opponents open the door to nuclear warfare while you spend your late-game shields on more beneficial Wonders. After all, you can build nuclear weapons too (should you need them) when someone else completes this Wonder.

Military Academy (Small Wonder)

Those who prefer to seek victory through war should note this inexpensive Small Wonder. If you're following the prescribed military research route, the Military Academy becomes available very early in the game, as soon as you discover Military Tradition and have at least five cities with Barracks.

This Wonder provides the only consistent way of producing Armies, greatly reducing your dependency on Leaders. Construct the Wonder in a central city so you can readily dispatch your Armies to any front.

Newton's University

The effects of this Wonder are identical to those of Copernicus's Observatory—except that Newton's University provides an extra Culture Point. The same advice that applies to Copernicus's Observatory applies to this Wonder: build it! When built in a city with high commerce, the research benefits are tremendous.

The Oracle

The Oracle is one of the more useful ancient Wonders, especially on higher difficulty levels. Even on lower difficulty levels, this Wonder eases the unrest that often results from rapid city growth. Use the Oracle-Temple combination to keep your citizens content in Ancient Times, and build Cathedrals in all of your cities before Theology cancels The Oracle's effects.

The Pentagon (Small Wonder)

The Pentagon goes hand-in-hand with the Heroic Epic and Military Academy Small Wonders, and the advice is essentially the same: This is an essential Wonder if you're seeking a Conquest Victory. Because you must have three Armies in the field to construct The Pentagon, you probably *are* following a military strategy—so build away! Strong Armies lead to swift victories.

The Pyramids

Rapid city growth early in the game can be a double-edged sword. The production gets your empire off to a rousing start but, if you grow too quickly, you run into unhappiness problems—especially on higher difficulty levels. Therefore, the same caveat that applies to building Granaries early in the game applies to The Pyramids.

If you like to build Granaries early, this Wonder offers you an economical solution to avoid the construction and maintenance costs of building Granaries in every city. It also gives you a nice early-game Culture boost.

> **NOTE**
> Like the updated versions of Hoover Dam and JS Bach's Cathedral, *Civ III*'s Pyramids only affect cities on the continent where the Wonder is built.

SETI Program

The effects of the updated SETI Program now mimic those of Copernicus's Observatory and Newton's University rather than acting as a Research Lab in all of your cities (as it did in *Civilization II*). That changes the inherent strategy for using the Wonder, though the new version still remains quite useful. Adding this Wonder to a commerce-rich city can provide just the late-game research boost you need to jump ahead of your opponents.

> **TIP**
> Want to build the ultimate research city? Build Copernicus's Observatory, Newton's University, and the SETI Program in a city that has a Library, a University, and a Research Lab.

Shakespeare's Theater

Shakespeare's Theater offers a dramatic effect with extremely limited scope. It's really more like a super-improvement than a Wonder. Despite the obvious local benefits of having a city with virtually no unhappiness, the limited scope of this Wonder makes it a low priority—especially when compared to other medieval Wonders such as JS Bach's Cathedral and the Sistine Chapel.

NOTE

The version of Shakespeare's Theater in *Civ III* is technically less powerful than the *Civ II* version—it only makes up to eight unhappy citizens in the city content rather than making *all* of them content. Of course, if you have more than eight unhappy citizens in one city, you've got serious problems anyway.

Sistine Chapel

This Wonder, formerly known as Michelangelo's Chapel, retains its importance in the rich assortment of medieval Wonders. Essentially, it is the medieval equivalent of The Oracle, doubling the effect of your Cathedrals where The Oracle Wonder affected temples.

Don't pass up this Wonder. The population control potential is huge and gives you a leg up on all of the unhappiness problems that come with city growth as you approach the Industrial Ages, especially on the higher difficulty levels.

Smith's Trading Company

As you know, most city improvements subtract maintenance costs from your treasury every turn. When you're strapped for cash due to a lack of commerce or an extended conflict, these fees can be devastating in a large empire.

If you anticipate this sort of situation—or if you just want a little extra cash in the coffers—build this Wonder. By eliminating the maintenance fees of your commerce-related improvements (Marketplaces, Banks, Harbors, and Airports), you could shave a great deal of Gold every turn in a large, well-developed empire. This Wonder provides a substantial Culture bonus, too.

Smith's Trading Company shouldn't take precedence over more significant medieval Wonders if you are forced to choose, but it's definitely worth building if you have the time and resources to spare.

Strategic Missile Defense (Small Wonder)

Civilization III has done away with the SDI Defense improvement and replaced it with this Small Wonder. The upside is that you no longer have to build an improvement in every individual city to protect it from nuclear attacks—one Wonder does it all! In fact, the level of protection is higher than it was for the old SDI Defense. The downside is that the protection for units surrounding the city has been eliminated.

As in *Civ II*, your enemies aren't shy about using nukes. Therefore, build this Wonder as soon as somebody builds The Manhattan Project. You'll be glad you did.

Sun Tzu's Art of War

This Wonder replaces Sun Tzu's War Academy from *Civ II*, and its effects have changed quite a bit. Sun Tzu's Art of War provides all of the Barracks benefits to each of your cities on the continent where the Wonder is built. This means you have fewer Barracks to build and maintain, and every unit you produce on that continent starts off with veteran status.

Sun Tzu's Art of War provides the greatest benefits if you're going for a Conquest Victory. Even so, if this Wonder is still available after you've completed the more compelling medieval Wonders, even pacifists should build it. Defensive units benefit from veteran status, too.

Theory of Evolution

Veteran players will remember this Wonder as Darwin's Voyage. They'll also remember that this Industrial Ages Wonder is not to be missed. Two free civilization advances are well worth the time and effort required. This is a huge, important boost at the start of the Industrial Ages, when the research costs start to increase dramatically.

The United Nations

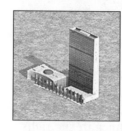

Although many Wonders with familiar names have changed in function since *Civ II*, none has changed more drastically than The United Nations. Once a tool to force peace and allow the easy waging of war under a Democracy, the UN is now a whole new beast.

As detailed in chapter IX, one way to win the game is by being elected leader of The United Nations. So, guess what? The Wonder has to be built before this is possible. Aside from the Culture you reap from it, that's the only reason to build this Wonder.

Universal Suffrage

This Wonder (formerly known as Women's Suffrage) still performs essentially the same function as its predecessor—it decreases population unhappiness due to ongoing military conflict. Specifically, it decreases the effect of war weariness on the population. (See chapter IV for more on war weariness.)

While an increase in Culture Points is always welcome, there's no compelling reason to produce this Wonder unless you're conducting a prolonged war (or expect to do so in the near future). The best way to deal with war weariness is to avoid warlike activities.

Wall Street (Small Wonder)

Wall Street is a gem of a Small Wonder that is available relatively early in the game. It becomes available once you have at least five cities with banks.

This Wonder is your civilization's answer to an IRA. The sooner you build this Wonder, the more benefits you'll reap from it. Other medieval Wonders are more important, so don't ignore them in favor of Wall Street. However, all that free money is just too good a deal to pass up for long.

VIII

UNITS AND COMBAT

Steady expansion is the key to success in the *Civilization® III* game—it's the cornerstone upon which every strategy is built. If you don't keep your empire's growth consistent with that of your opponents, your science and Culture will suffer and you can fall prey to a hostile neighbor. Fall too far behind and you'll never catch up. You must grow to prosper, and your units are the key to both expanding your empire and protecting it from your enemies.

The first few sections describe all the units in the game—including the new civilization-specific units, Leaders, and Armies—and the strategies associated with them. The last section of the chapter

discusses the combat system in *Civ® III* and some of the more effective strategies that will help you survive both offensive and defensive combat situations.

> ## CAUTION
> **Although many of the units in *Civilization III* share the names of their *Civilization II* counterparts, many of their vital statistics, such as attack and defense strength, have changed drastically. Don't assume that your established strategies involving units will still work. Browse this chapter for important information on changes and new unit strategies.**

GROUND UNITS

Units come in three basic forms—ground, naval, and air. By far the most common are ground units and, accordingly, they embody a wide variety of functions, from basic combat and defense duties to terrain development and city building.

Table 8-1 lists the statistics of the standard ground units. The following statistics are listed for each unit:

- **Cost:** The number of shields it takes to build the unit.

- **ADM:** Shorthand for "Attack," "Defense," and "Movement." For example, a unit with an ADM of "2.4.1" has an attack strength of 2, a defensive strength of 4, and can move 1 map square per turn.

- **BRF:** Shorthand for the new concepts of "Bombardment Power," "(Operational) Range," and "(Rate of) Fire." A unit with a BRF of "8.1.2" has a bombardment power of 8, can launch bombardments from 1 square away (the adjacent square), and fires 2 shots per bombardment.

- **Prerequisite:** The civilization advance you must discover before you can build the unit.

- **Strategic Resources Required:** The strategic resource(s) a city must have access to before building the unit.

TABLE 8-1. GROUND UNIT STATISTICS

UNIT	COST	ADM	BRF	PREREQUISITE	STRATEGIC RESOURCES REQUIRED
Archer	20	2.1.1	—	Warrior Code	—
Artillery	60	0.0.1	12.2.3	Replaceable Parts	—
Cannon	40	0.0.1	8.1.2	Metallurgy	Saltpeter, Iron
Catapult	20	0.0.1	4.1.1	Mathematics	—
Cavalry	80	6.3.3	—	Military Tradition	Horses, Saltpeter
Chariot	20	1.1.2	—	The Wheel	Horses
Explorer	20	1.1.2	—	Navigation	—
Horseman	30	2.1.2	—	Horseback Riding	Horses
Infantry	90	8.12.2	—	Replaceable Parts	—
Knight	70	4.3.2	—	Chivalry	Horses, Iron

continued on next page

TABLE 8-1. GROUND UNIT STATISTICS, CONTINUED

UNIT	COST	ADM	BRF	PREREQUISITE	STRATEGIC RESOURCES REQUIRED
Longbowman	40	4.1.1	—	Invention	—
Marine	100	10.8.1	—	Amphibious War	Rubber
Mech Infantry	110	12.20.3	—	Computers	Oil, Rubber
Modern Armor	120	24.16.3	—	Synthetic Fibers	Oil, Rubber, Aluminum
Musketman	60	2.4.1	—	Gunpowder	Saltpeter
Paratrooper	100	8.10.1	—	Advanced Flight	Oil, Rubber
Pikeman	30	1.3.1	—	Feudalism	Iron
Radar Artillery	80	0.0.1	16.2.4	Robotics	Aluminum
Rifleman	80	4.6.1	—	Nationalism	—
Settler	30*	0.0.1	—	—	—
Spearman	20	1.2.1	—	Bronze Working	—
Swordsman	30	3.2.1	—	Iron Working	Iron
Tank	100	16.10.2	—	Motorized Transportation	Oil, Rubber
Warrior	10	1.1.1	—	—	—
Worker	10**	0.0.1	—	—	—

* Plus 2 points of the city's population
** Plus 1 point of the city's population

Archer

Archers are the best attack unit available in the pre–Iron Working world. It's not a bad idea to have an Archer or two around to deal with Barbarians and any other enemies who might harass you early on.

TIP

Civilization II *veterans should note: Archers are no longer the stalwart defenders they once were. If you don't start out with Bronze Working, pursue that first so that you can build Spearmen to defend your cities. In the early game, a strong offense is* not *the best defense.*

Artillery

Many units have completely changed their method of attack thanks to the new bombardment rules (described later in this chapter). Artillery is one of the affected units.

Artillery takes over where Cannons leave off, acting as a precursor to your invasion forces' direct attack on a city by softening it up with bombardment. Artillery is a little safer than its predecessors in the field because it doesn't have to be adjacent to its target to launch its attack.

> **TIP**
>
> *Because they have no way to defend themselves, artillery-type units can be captured simply by moving any military unit into their square. (They do get one free shot at the attacking enemy, but there is little chance that they can avoid capture in this manner.) For this reason, never send artillery units into the field unescorted. Leave at least one strong defensive unit in the square with the artillery unit at all times.*

Cannon

The ancestors of Artillery and the descendants of Catapults, Cannons serve the same purpose as these other bombarding units. As is the case in Ancient Times, bombardment in the Middle Ages can help ease your unit loss when you're attacking a city. If a Cannon manages to take out the city's defensive units and/or Walls, your direct-attack units' jobs will be a little easier.

Catapult

Catapults in the previous *Civilization* games used to be a license to wreak havoc on your neighbors. Most really big early-game military strategies began after the discovery of Mathematics.

Now that Catapults are bombardment units only, they're not suited to solo attack roles. They are, however, still very useful in early attack strategies. When possible, precede any attack on an enemy city with a couple turns of Catapult bombardment. Softening the enemy defenses is vital in the Middle Ages because of your units' relatively weak offensive power.

Cavalry

Cavalry represents mounted troops of the 19th century, and their advances over both Horsemen and Knights is obvious the moment you begin using them. If you're following a warlike path, Cavalry is *the* attack unit of the Middle Ages. Watch out for cities defended by Pikemen, though—Pikemen are especially effective at repelling mounted units.

Chariot

The Chariots in *Civ III* are considerably less powerful on the attack than the Chariots in previous games, but they have a new advantage, one that is shared by no other unit this early in the game—the ability to retreat from battle. This ability, combined with the Chariot's speed, makes it extremely useful early in the game—at least until Horsemen become available.

NOTE

Keep in mind that access to strategic resources is required to build many units. It's no longer a foregone conclusion that you can build a unit just because you've researched its prerequisite advance.

Explorer

Explorers can be extremely useful for, well, exploration. Explorers can cover three squares a turn in any terrain, so if you're on a big continent with lots of unexplored space early on, the fastest way to learn the lay of the land—and, perhaps, get some "goodies"—is to send out an Explorer or two. Just be aware that these units seldom survive any opposition.

Horseman

Horsemen have a definite attack advantage over Chariots, the other "fast" unit of Ancient Times, and they share the same ability to retreat from combat when they're losing. However, their combat ability is pretty weak. They make decent exploration units (when you need something beefier than an Explorer), but they're not much when it comes to launching an invasion. Research Chivalry so you can upgrade your Horsemen to Knights.

Infantry

This unit, new to *Civilization III*, is an intermediate step between Riflemen and Mech Infantry. Nothing on land beats it for its defensive capabilities during the Industrial Ages. This unit is important enough that you should discover Replaceable Parts as early as possible so that you can skip Riflemen altogether. Upgrade all your city garrisons to Infantry as soon as you can.

Knight

Knights are, essentially, the first armor unit, and they are a huge improvement over their ancestors, the Horsemen. In a nonmilitary strategy, it's easy to overlook Knights. Chivalry need not be researched to move on to any of the other medieval advances, so it's often overlooked. If you're out to conquer the world, you *must* take the time for Chivalry so that you can build Knights. Otherwise, your military will suffer throughout the Middle Ages.

Longbowman

The newly introduced Longbowman is a double-strength Archer that becomes available early in the Middle Ages. While this unit packs an offensive punch, in practice, you'll seldom use it. Aside from its offensive capabilities, the only advantage of Longbowmen is that they require no special resources to build—a rarity among medieval units.

The better-balanced Musketman and the powerful Knights make better choices for offensive units during this time period.

Marine

Marines are among the most effective attack units of the Industrial Ages. With an offensive strength rivaled only by Tanks, these units would be formidable even without their most important capability: amphibious assault. Marines are the only units that can attack enemy units and cities directly from a ship—just unload them in the enemy's terrain square and combat commences. This combined with their impressive defensive strength makes Marines ideal for taking and holding enemy coastal cities.

Mech Infantry

Mech Infantry is, hands down, the best defensive unit in the game. Nothing can rival its ability to protect a city. Its relatively high attack makes it versatile enough to act as an offensive unit in a pinch, but defense should be this unit's primary role.

NOTE

Because it was off the beaten research path in *Civilization II*, you had to deviate from your chosen research path to gain Mech Infantry. Now that this unit is made possible through the discovery of Computers, there's no excuse not to upgrade your defenders to Mech Infantry in Modern Times.

Modern Armor

In previous versions of *Civilization*, the Armor unit (now known as the "Tank") was the ultimate land-based fighting machine. In *Civ III*, there's one final upgrade—and oh what an upgrade it is.

Modern Armor has 33 percent more attack strength and significantly more defensive capabilities than its Industrial Ages counterpart. Indispensable to a conquest strategy, Modern Armor can crush just about anything that gets in its way. If you're going for world domination, upgrade your Tanks ASAP and roll out the Modern Armor. Victory is in sight!

Musketman

Musketmen are the rough equivalent of "Musketeers" from the previous *Civilization* games—though Musketeers appear in this game as well, as units exclusive to the French.

This is primarily a defensive unit, and it performs well in that role. As soon as you discover Gunpowder, make sure that your cities have access to Saltpeter and upgrade all of your defenders to Musketmen as soon as possible. They are the strongest defense available in the Middle Ages.

Paratrooper

Paratroopers, like Marines, have a unique ability. They can airdrop directly to a target square from any city equipped with an Airport. They have a decent attack factor and a very strong defense which, combined with their airdrop capabilities, leads to an interesting strategy for taking control of enemy cities (described later in this chapter). Paratroopers are also on par with the best defenders of the Industrial Ages. It is sometimes worth the extra cost (over Infantry) to place Paratrooper defenders in your border cities that are within airdrop distance of opposing cities.

Pikeman

Pikemen are among the best defenders available prior to the discovery of Gunpowder. Their defensive power is slightly higher than their predecessors (Spearmen) and they receive a bonus when defending against mounted units—an important factor in the Middle Ages, when Knights and other mounted units become prevalent. As soon as you can, upgrade your defensive units to Pikemen.

Radar Artillery

Radar Artillery is the most advanced artillery unit in the game. Its bombardment power is unrivaled—even Battleships can't match its awesome damage potential. Like Artillery, it can launch its bombardment from a range of two squares.

Although you won't use this unit much if you're pursuing a peaceful victory, a vanguard of Radar Artillery is just the ticket for quick and easy subjugation of enemy cities for you warmongers.

Rifleman

It's worth pursuing Nationalism immediately upon entering the Industrial Ages just to gain access to the Rifleman. This unit improves upon its predecessors, making it a much more effective defender than the earlier Musketmen. Another advantage is that you don't need access to Saltpeter to build them. Say goodbye to the Musketmen and upgrade your defensive units to Riflemen ASAP. They're the best defenders you have until the discovery of Replaceable Parts allows you to build Infantry much later in the Industrial Ages.

Settler

Whether you're a militant conqueror or a mild-mannered pursuer of science, the Settler is one of the two most important units early in the game. Only Settlers can build cities, and without new cities, your empire can't expand. Later in the

game, you'll gain cities through conquest and defection, rendering the Settler less useful, but throughout Ancient Times and the Middle Ages, few units are more useful.

NOTE

It costs more than shields to build Settlers and Workers. When a city builds a Settler, the city's population is reduced by two. When a city builds a Worker, its population is reduced by one. Therefore, build Settlers and Workers only in cities with a population of three or more.

Spearman

This unit makes your Warriors obsolete. They aren't a whole lot better, but they're the best defenders available in Ancient Times. Spend the extra production time on these units. Warriors are adequate defenders for your first few cities, but they can't withstand much punishment if you should meet a hostile neighbor early in the game.

Swordsman

Swordsmen become available as soon as you discover Iron Working. When you look at their stats, you might be tempted to use them as city defenders rather than the offensively-weaker Spearmen. While this works fine in the short run, the flaw in this strategy is that Swordsmen, unlike Spearmen, cannot be upgraded to Pikemen. That means that you have to build new defenders from scratch when you need to upgrade, and that's expensive.

Use Swordsmen exclusively for offensive missions, where they outclass just about every other ancient unit available.

Tank

Tanks used to be called "Armor." Regardless of what you call it, this is an extremely important unit to any offensive strategy.

Tanks attack with a power unrivaled in units of their time. They can launch multiple attacks in a single turn, and they are "fast units"—which means they can retreat from an attack when they're losing. Tanks are adequate defenders, capable of holding a captured enemy city if need be. However, less expensive and more effective defenders (Infantry, for example) are better choices in strictly defensive roles.

Warrior

Warriors are strictly "stone knives and bearskins" units. In certain cases, they're they only units you can build (besides Settlers and Workers) early in the game. Only under these circumstances, or when you need a city defender quickly, should you *ever* bother building a Warrior. Spearmen make better defenders and Swordsman make better attackers—and both are available very early in the game.

Worker

The Settlers in *Civ III* have it easy—all they do is build cities. All of the other traditional Settler duties—roads, mining, irrigation, and so on—are now performed by Workers. This makes Workers and Settlers equally important at the start of the game. As the game progresses, Settlers become less vital, but Workers retain their usefulness right to the end.

The best advice about Workers is to build as many as you can and keep them busy. Set them on automatic and let them toil endlessly to improve your terrain and build an infrastructure of roads and (later) railroads to keep your trade brisk and fruitful.

AUTOMATED WORKERS

Although the automate feature for Workers is excellent, don't let it lull you into not keeping tabs on them. Two things to watch for:

- When they run out of things to do, Workers enter a nearby city and sit there until you manually reactivate them.

- When they finish working in your territory, automated Workers often start building roads to your opponents' cities. This is great for trade, but be careful! If you don't have a right-of-passage treaty with your neighbors, your innocent Workers might be considered a hostile incursion.

Keep an eye on your automated Workers and redirect them when they start doing things you don't want them to do. Or use the limited automation controls (listed in the manual) to confine the Worker to a specific area or set of tasks.

IMPASSIBLE TERRAIN

In *Civ III*, some units cannot pass through certain terrain types. This has always been true of water squares—ground units can't pass through them and naval units can't move on any thing *but* them. Now, some land squares are considered impassible to a handful of ground units.

The following unit types cannot pass through Jungle or Mountain terrain unless a road has been built through it:

- Artillery
- Cannon
- Catapult
- Modern Armor
- Panzer
- Radar Artillery
- Tank

NAVAL UNITS

In the average game, you'll build a lot fewer naval units than you will ground units—but that doesn't mean that naval units aren't important! Early in the game, naval units provide the mobility to quickly explore the world and transport units to different continents. Later in the game, especially if you're following a military strategy, naval units are invaluable. They give you the transport and bombardment capabilities you need to make your conquest efforts swift and effective.

Table 8-2 lists the statistics of all standard naval units. The statistics shown are the same as those in table 8-1, except that a fourth number (T) is added to some units' ADM statistic. This indicates the number of units it is capable of transporting. For example, "1.1.3(2)" shows 1 attack, 1 defense, 3 movement, and the ability to transport 2 units.

TABLE 8-2. NAVAL UNIT STATISTICS

UNIT	COST	ADM(T)	BRF	PREREQUISITE	STRATEGIC RESOURCES
AEGIS Cruiser	160	12.12.6	4.2.4	Robotics	Aluminum, Uranium
Battleship	200	24.20.4	8.2.4	Mass Production	Oil
Caravel	40	1.2.3(4)	—	Astronomy	—
Carrier	180	1.8.4(4*)	—	Mass Production	Oil
Destroyer	120	16.12.6	6.1.3	Combustion	Oil
Frigate	60	2.2.4	2.1.2	Magnetism	Iron, Saltpeter
Galleon	60	1.2.4(6)	—	Magnetism	—

continued on next page

TABLE 8-2. NAVAL UNIT STATISTICS, CONTINUED

UNIT	COST	ADM(T)	BRF	PREREQUISITE	STRATEGIC RESOURCES
Galley	30	1.1.3(2)	—	Map Making	—
Ironclad	80	4.4.3	4.1.2	Steam Power	Iron, Coal
Nuclear Submarine	120	4.4.3(1**)	—	Fission	Uranium
Privateer	50	1.1.3	—	Magnetism	Iron, Saltpeter
Submarine	100	6.4.3	—	Mass Production	Oil
Transport	100	1.4.4(8)	—	Combustion	Oil

* Air units only

** Tactical Nukes only

AEGIS Cruiser

One of the most formidable naval vessels in the game, the AEGIS Cruiser's bombardment and attack power, combined with its longer visual range and ability to spot submarines, make it a valuable addition to a naval-intensive strategy. AEGIS Cruisers are particularly useful as escorts for weaker ships and Transports.

Battleship

The offensive and defensive power of Battleships is unmatched by any other sea unit, as is its bombardment capability. This versatility makes the Battleship a force to contend with in both traditional combat and bombardment scenarios. Despite the availability of powerful ground-based artillery units, Battleship bombardment is the best way to soften up any coastal (or near-coastal) enemy city prior to traditional invasion.

Caravel

Caravels are the first naval units with real exploratory power. Their combat ability is quite limited, but they can usually defend themselves in a skirmish. (Don't consider waging naval warfare until you at least have some Frigates in your fleet.) The real boon of the Caravel is its transport capacity, which is a significant improvement over that of a Galley.

NOTE

Caravels in *Civ III* suffer from a weakness that they didn't have in the previous games: the inability to traverse Ocean squares. Until the discovery of Navigation, Caravels must end their turn in a Coast or Sea square or run the risk of being lost at sea.

Carrier

Carriers are the most formidable vessels in the real world. They are also quite powerful in *Civ III*, but not on their own. Their power lies in the air units they transport. Carriers provide a mobile base for Bombers and Stealth Bombers, giving you the ability to launch lethal bombardments on multiple targets simultaneously.

Carriers with their attendant air wings are quite expensive. Because this unit's defensive power is comparatively low, a defensive escort (such as an AEGIS Cruiser) should always share the same terrain square.

Destroyer

Destroyers are cost-effective naval attackers that provide a cheap way to boost your naval power. Their speed makes them effective hit-and-run raiders but, despite their adequate attack and bombardment capabilities, their relatively low defensive value makes Destroyers unsuited for prolonged naval conflicts.

Frigate

Magnetism provides the biggest single jump in naval power in the game. Of all of the ships it makes possible, the Frigate is the best suited for naval warfare. Although it lacks significant traditional attack capabilities, it can launch fairly powerful bombardments on coastal cities. Frigates are much more mobile than ground artillery for this task.

NOTE

Unlike the Frigates in *Civilization II*, the Frigates in *Civ III* cannot transport ground units.

Galleon

Like Frigates, Galleons become available with the discovery of Magnetism. These units are totally unsuited for warfare—they're barely able to defend themselves. Their strength lies in their ability to transport a large number of ground units, making their role vital in both colonization and warfare. Galleons should be accompanied by a military vessel (such as a Frigate) at all times, especially during war.

Galley

Galleys are the first naval units available in the game. Like their predecessors from previous *Civ* games (Triremes), they get lost at sea if they don't end their turn adjacent to land. Despite their weaknesses, these units are vital to early exploration, especially if the world is made up of lots of small landmasses. They are totally unsuited to warfare, but as transports and explorers they're adequate until Caravels become available.

NOTE

The Great Lighthouse Wonder allows Galleys to end their movement in a Sea square, but they are still lost if they end their movement in an Ocean square.

Ironclad

Though slower than Frigates, Ironclads provide a considerable offensive and defensive edge in traditional combat, as well as a considerable increase in bombardment power. If your strategy requires naval superiority, Ironclads are a must, even though Destroyers quickly surpass them in power and versatility later in the Industrial Ages.

Nuclear Submarine

Nuclear Submarines have the same stealth capabilities as their Submarine predecessors and possess the same attack, defense, and movement capabilities. What makes the Nuclear version so special is its ability to carry a single Tactical Nuke onboard. This allows you to sneak a nuclear weapon to within striking distance of an enemy coastal city undetected! If you decide to dabble in the dirty business of nuclear war, Nuclear Submarines are a must.

NOTE

Nuclear Submarines are analogous to standard Submarines in the previous *Civilization* games, although their attack capabilities have been significantly reduced.

Privateer

At first glance, Privateers are rather unspectacular warships—especially when compared to Frigates, which become available at the same time. What's unique about this unit is that it allows you to attack your neighbors without fear of reprisal. Privateers don't reveal their nationality! While the low attack and defense factor of Privateers makes them impractical for prolonged warfare, they're just the things to pick off enemy Galleons that are transporting unwanted opposing troops into your territory.

Submarine

The main role for Submarines is protecting cities and shipping lanes from unwanted sea traffic. The stealth capabilities of Submarines allow them to attack enemy ships before they know what hit them. Only after AEGIS Cruisers and Aircraft Carriers become prevalent is this advantage lost. Even if you follow a nonmilitary strategy, you benefit from a few Submarines to help keep your waters safe from intruders.

TIP

Submarines are great for setting up naval blockades of enemy port cities. By blocking the direct path to a city with a Harbor, you cut off that city's trade with other Harbor-equipped cities. Submarines, with their stealth capabilities, can set up a blockade that goes unnoticed for some time. Simply park a Submarine in every water square that leads out of the city—three is usually sufficient, depending on how many Coast squares touch the city.

Transport

Although Transports can now initiate combat, they never should. The sole purpose of this unit is transporting ground units across the water. Because of their relatively low defensive capabilities, a naval unit with decent attack and defense values should always escort Transports. Remember—when a Transport is destroyed, so do all of the units inside. Transports carrying Marines are particularly adept at taking cities.

AIR UNITS

Air units comprise the smallest category of units. This is primarily because they become available so late in the game.

Players who are out to conquer the world benefit most from these units, because most of them (except the Helicopter) are strictly military.

Civilization III introduces an entirely new method of operation for air units. Instead of moving like normal units, they fly missions from a centralized base (usually a city) and return to that base when the mission is complete.

Table 8-3 lists the statistics of all standard air units. The statistics shown are the same as those in table 8-2, with a slight change to the BRF stat. Many air units technically have an Operational Range of zero—they cannot leave their home city. When a number is shown in parenthesis, it indicates the maximum distance from their home city at which they can perform missions.

TABLE 8-3. AIR UNIT STATISTICS

UNIT	COST	ADM(T)	BRF	PREREQUISITE	STRATEGIC RESOURCES
Bomber	100	0.2.0	8.0(6).3	Flight	Oil
Cruise Missile	40	0.0.1	20.4.6	Rocketry	Aluminum
Fighter	80	4.4.0	2.0(4).2	Flight	Oil
Helicopter	80	0.4.0(2)	0.0(4).0	Advanced Flight	Oil, Rubber
ICBM	300	0.0.1	—	Space Flight	Aluminum, Uranium
Jet Fighter	100	8.8.0	2.0(6).1	Rocketry	Oil
Stealth Bomber	140	0.2.0	8.0(8).4	Stealth	Oil, Aluminum
Stealth Fighter	120	0.4.0	2.0(6).2	Stealth	Oil, Aluminum
Tactical Nuke	200	0.0.1	—	Space Flight	Aluminum, Uranium

Bomber

Bombers are the best source of quick, repetitive bombardments of an enemy target. Their ability in this regard is surpassed only by Stealth Bombers, to which normal Bombers can be upgraded after the discovery of Stealth. Because of their range of operation and the less-vulnerable nature of air units in general, Bombers are far superior to any ground artillery bombardments when dealing with enemy targets near your borders.

Cruise Missile

Cruise Missiles are, essentially, one-use airborne artillery pieces. They provide a cheap, effective means of bombarding enemy cities as a precursor to a traditional attack. Unlike ground-based artillery, Cruise Missiles are not limited by terrain. Their only limitation is their operational range, which is much shorter than that of Bombers. Cruise Missiles are most effective when launched from Carriers, which can get the Cruise Missiles closer to a wider variety of targets.

Fighter

Fighters and other Fighter-type air units are much more versatile in *Civ III* than they were in the previous games. In addition to their air-to-air capabilities, Fighters can now execute Bomber-type missions as well.

Fighters operate from a fixed base. Because their range is more limited than that of Bombers, Fighters tend to be more effective in an offensive role when they are Carrier based and can be delivered to within range of more potential targets.

Helicopter

The Helicopter's role has changed quite a bit since *Civilization II*. Whereas they used to be powerful attack units, they are now useless in that capacity. Their new role, however, is nearly as important.

Helicopters now act as transports. That's right—now, you can transport ground units by air rather than by sea. There are only a couple of drawbacks. First, a Helicopter's range is limited. Second, Helicopters cannot carry mechanized units (Tanks, Mech Infantry, and so on). Even so, Helicopters can be extremely useful.

CAUTION

Don't drop troops from a Helicopter into a square that is occupied by an enemy unit. If you do, the units you drop are automatically lost.

ICBM

The ICBM (Inter-Continental Ballistics Missile, although it's never referred to formally in the game) takes the place of the Nuclear Missile unit found in *Civilization II*. It is essentially the same unit, but with significantly improved destructive qualities. ICBMs don't move like normal units. Instead, they can target any square on the world map and instantly deliver their attack upon launch.

ICBMs have a 50 percent chance of killing every unit in their target square and in the eight surrounding squares immediately, and cause a reduction in city population (if a city is targeted). Launching ICBMs is a sure way to turn world opinion against you. Then again, you probably won't be using nukes if you care what other civilizations think.

Jet Fighter

Jet Fighters are more powerful versions of standard Fighters. They have the operational range of a Bomber, but nowhere near the Bomber's bombardment capabilities. They also can "see" two squares in any direction, regardless of terrain. This makes them good reconnaissance units. Like Fighters, Jet Fighters are most versatile when operated off of Carriers.

Stealth Bomber

Stealth Bombers are Bombers with extended range and a couple of notable advantages. They are less susceptible to interception by other aircraft and SAM

Batteries than their non-stealth counterparts. More importantly, they can carry out precision strikes against enemy cities, destroying a specific improvement of your choice. This is a great way to throw enemy cities into chaos. For example, by destroying a Cathedral, you can cause rampant unhappiness and civil unrest.

Stealth Fighter

Stealth Fighters are the ultimate air fighter craft. They retain all of the abilities of Jet Fighters and have the added abilities of Fighter/SAM Battery resistance and precision strike capability. It's worth the cost to upgrade your Jet Fighters to the stealth version if only to make them more difficult to destroy.

Tactical Nuke

Tactical Nukes are similar to ICBMs, and the diplomatic consequences for their use are pretty much the same. If you ever intend to change your warlike ways and try for a peaceful victory, don't use nuclear weapons. The negative impact on the opposing leaders' opinion of you is difficult to overcome.

CIVILIZATION-SPECIFIC UNITS

A new factor that sets the civilizations apart in *Civ III* is the inclusion of units that can be built only by specific civilizations. In most cases, these units are more powerful versions of units that can be built by other civilizations. The type of unit and the age in which it becomes available vary from tribe to tribe, as do the advantages they impart.

As discussed in chapter II, when you choose which civilization you want to play, you should familiarize yourself with that civilization's unique unit. That way, you can choose the civilization whose unique unit best suits your style of play.

Table 8-4 lists the statistics of the civilization-specific units. The statistics are the same as those shown in table 8-3 with the exception of the following:

- **Civilization:** The civilization(s) allowed to build the unit.

TABLE 8-4. CIVILIZATION-SPECIFIC UNITS STATISTICS

UNIT	CIVILIZATION	COST	ADM	BRF	PREREQUISITE	STRATEGIC RESOURCES
Bowman	Babylonians	20	2.1.2	—	Warrior Code	—
Cossack	Russians	80	6.4.3	—	Military Tradition	Horses, Saltpeter
F-15	Americans	100	10.8.0	2.0(6).1	Rocketry	Oil
Hoplite	Greeks	20	1.3.1	—	Bronze Working	—
Immortals	Persian	30	4.2.1	—	Iron Working	Iron
Impi	Zulu	20	1.2.2	—	Bronze Working	—
Jaguar Warrior	Aztecs	10	1.1.2	—	—	—
Legionary	Romans	30	3.3.1	—	Iron Working	Iron
Man-O-War	English	60	3.2.4	2.1.2	Magnetism	Iron, Saltpeter
Mounted Warrior	Iroquois	30	3.1.2	—	Horseback Riding	Horses
Musketeer	French	60	3.4.1	—	Gunpowder	Saltpeter
Panzer	Germans	100	16.10.3	—	Motorized Transportation	Oil, Rubber
Rider	Chinese	70	4.4.3	—	Feudalism	Horses, Iron

continued on next page

TABLE 8-4. CIVILIZATION-SPECIFIC UNITS STATISTICS, CONTINUED

UNIT	CIVILIZATION	COST	ADM	BRF	PREREQUISITE	STRATEGIC RESOURCES
Samurai	Japanese	80	4.4.2	—	Chivalry	Iron
Scout	Americans, Zulu, Iroquois, Russians, English	10	0.0.2	—	—	—
War Chariot	Egyptians	20	2.1.2	—	The Wheel	Horses
War Elephant	Indians	70	4.3.2	—	Chivalry	—

Bowman (Babylonians)

The Babylonian Bowman gives you a tactical offensive advantage in Ancient Times. While its attack value is the same as that of the Archer, it moves at twice the Archer's speed. This allows you to move into attack position more quickly than your neighbors. It also allows the Bowman to retreat when losing a battle—an advantage that helps to keep your military units from being needlessly lost at the beginning of the game, when you can least afford to lose them.

Cossack (Russians)

The Russian Cossacks share all of the advantages of the standard Cavalry unit, but sport a higher defensive value. This gives the Russians a military edge when it comes to mounted unit combat in the Middle Ages and early Industrial Ages. When playing the Russians, you're likely to exploit a unit to great effect.

F-15 (Americans)

The F-15 is identical to the Jet Fighter but has a significantly increased operational range. Of all of the civ-specific units, this one appears latest in the game.

Whether or not you benefit from this unit depends on your style of play. If your strategy depends on maintaining air superiority over your neighbors, the F-15 gives you a definite edge. Otherwise, don't choose the Americans—you'd benefit more from the special units provided by other civilizations.

Hoplite (Greeks)

If your strategy is a peaceful one, solid defensive units are one of the keys to your success—although the Greek Hoplite might arrive a little early in the game to do you a whole lot of good. It replaces the Spearman, providing you with an early defensive advantage. When you're playing on a small world or on higher difficulty levels, this can be quite helpful. Otherwise, it's likely that you'll be well beyond Hoplites before you have to worry too much about defending your cities from attack.

> **TIP**
>
> *Aggressive strategies often involve conquering as many civilizations as possible early in the game, before they have a chance to spread and grow strong. If you're following such a strategy, beware of the Greeks in Ancient Times. Hoplites are more than capable of dealing with whatever you throw at them early on. You're better off making friends with the Greeks and concentrate your efforts elsewhere until you have more powerful offensive units at your disposal.*

Impi (Zulu)

Impis are an odd mix of abilities. They are, essentially, fast Spearmen. That means they can retreat from combat quickly when they're losing. Of course, tactical retreat capabilities best serve offensive units—which, obviously, the Impi is not. Of the Ancient civ-specific units, Impis are the least effective.

Immortal (Persians)

Immortals are the Persians' answer to Swordsmen. Their advantage is purely offensive—their attack value is the highest of any Ancient Times unit available. Like the Babylonian Bowman, this unit is most beneficial if you are following an early aggressive strategy. Of all of the civilizations in the game, the Persians are the most likely to gain military dominance early in the game by swiftly taking out their closest neighbors with their bands of Immortals.

> **TIP**
>
> *If you find yourself near the Persians during Ancient Times, do your best to stay on friendly terms with them. If you anger them, their Immortals can cause you a great deal of heartache and, possibly, cost you the game.*

Jaguar Warrior (Aztecs)

The advantage the Aztecs gain with their Jaguar Warrior is short-lived. This unit is a faster version of the Warrior. While the ability to move faster and retreat from battle gives this unit an edge over standard Warriors, even the short-term usefulness is questionable, because Jaguar Warriors aren't really powerful enough to make them effective attackers. Probably the best use for this unit is exploration—they're faster than Scouts and can defend themselves.

Legionary (Romans)

The Roman Legionary is a rarity in that it is equally adept at attack and defense. Like the Swordsman that it replaces, the Legionary cannot be upgraded to the next best defender (the Pikeman) as Spearmen can—you have to build the new defender from scratch. However, because of this unit's excellent defensive value, the tradeoff is worth the cost, especially if you're plagued with hostile neighbors at the start of the game. The dual nature of their special unit makes the Romans a good civilization choice for both peaceful and warlike strategies.

Man-O-War (English)

The English are the only civilization whose special unit is a naval unit. If naval warfare is your thing, consider playing the English. With advantages in both conventional and bombardment attacks, the Man-O-War rules the seas in the late Middle Ages and early Industrial Ages.

NOTE

The Man-O-War's reign can be quite short-lived depending on your opponents' research paths. It is bested by the Ironclad, which can be discovered quite soon after Magnetism (the advance that makes the Man-O-War available).

Mounted Warrior (Iroquois)

The Iroquois have an early advantage when it comes to mounted units. Horsemen as a general rule are not all that effective, especially when it comes to attacking cities. The extra attack strength of the Mounted Warrior gives this unit the extra push it needs to prevail in many combat situations. Even so, Mounted Warriors still lack strong defensive capabilities, a weakness they share with Horsemen. Mounted Warriors do make good scout units early in the game.

Musketeer (French)

Musketeers enjoy a better attack statistic than Musketmen, giving the French a more versatile unit than their opponents after the discovery of Gunpowder. While they are still no match for Knights when it comes to offensive actions, Musketeers are more likely to prevail in an attack than Musketmen—a plus when following an aggressive strategy.

Panzer (Germans)

The German Panzer is, arguably, the best available civilization-specific unit. It beats the Tank in both defensive power and movement rate, making it a truly formidable attack *and* defense unit. Some of the most decisive aggressive activity takes place starting in the late Industrial Ages. If your strategy usually involves rolling over your opponents as soon as you have Tanks, play the Germans. Panzers make your job easier.

Rider (Chinese)

The Rider provides the Chinese with a double advantage. It's an improved (better defense and better movement) version of the Knight, an already powerful unit, and

it's available after the discovery of Feudalism. This is significant, because it means that the Chinese player doesn't have to take the time to research Chivalry. You get a powerful unit and a research shortcut, just for playing the Chinese! If you like to establish military dominance early in the game, the Rider gives you that opportunity.

Samurai (Japanese)

The Japanese (along with the Chinese and the Indians) have a special unit that replaces the Knight. The Samurai improves upon the Knight's defensive power, making for a more well-rounded unit. Although they don't share the research and movement advantages of Riders (as described earlier), Samurai are still a formidable replacement for an already formidable unit.

Scout

Scouts are unique in that they are limited not to a single civilization but to five of them—American, English, Iroquois, Russian, and Zulu.

Essentially, this unit is an early, less-powerful Explorer. They offer an early-game exploratory advantage to these five civilizations, a real boon especially when playing on a large world.

> ## NOTE
> The civilizations that can build Scouts usually start the game with three units—a Settler, a Worker, and a Scout—rather than the usual two. That makes these civilizations good choices if your strategy includes lots of early expansion and exploration. It also gives you a better opportunity to quickly find a "perfect" site for your first city.

War Chariot (Egyptians)

Veteran players quickly realize that the normal Chariot in *Civ III* doesn't quite have the "teeth" that its predecessors had. If you miss the old Chariot, you can still use it—but only if you play the Egyptians. This unit gives you all of the fast-attack/retreat advantages of the normal Chariot with an improved attack value, which makes it powerful enough to effectively attack cities as well as other units. As an added bonus, War Chariots upgrade directly to Knights (as opposed to standard Chariots, which upgrade to Horsemen). The Egyptians are a good choice if you want to gain an early military dominance over your neighbors.

War Elephant (Indians)

Like Chinese Riders and Japanese Samurai, Indian War Elephants take the place of Knights. Of these three similar units, the War Elephant is the only one that doesn't offer any statistical advantage over the Knight. The advantage here is that no strategic resources are required to build the unit. This means that all of your cities can build the unit. This can give you a definite advantage, especially if you're operating in an area with limited strategic resources.

LEADERS AND ARMIES

Leaders and Armies add a new dimension of combat to *Civilization III*. Neither is a unit in the traditional sense, though both share certain traits with them.

When an elite unit wins a battle, there is a 1 in 16 chance that the unit will turn into a Leader. Leaders have neither attack or defense values—all they can do is move. Luckily, they can move pretty quickly because, when a Leader appears, you want to get him to one of your cities as quickly as possible.

NOTE

After you build the Heroic Epic Small Wonder, the chance of an elite unit turning into a Leader after a victory is increased to 1 in 12.

After you move a Leader into your city, there are two things the Leader can do:

- **Complete an improvement or Wonder:** If the city is building an improvement or Wonder, the Leader can be sacrificed to complete its production in one turn.

- **Form an Army:** The leader can be transformed into an Army "unit."

Unless you already have too many Armies in the field—you can only have one for every four cities—or you simply have no need for an Army, chances are that most of your Leaders will be used for Army formation.

TIP

If you're using your Leaders to complete great works, it's worth switching a city to Wonder production just before the Leader arrives there. The Leader completes the Wonder in one turn no matter how far along it is in its production.

Armies are essentially transport shells that allow you to group three units (four if you've built The Pentagon Wonder) into a single attack unit. These units still fight

and defend as individuals, but they gain an interesting advantage. Armies share the hit points of all of the units inside.(See the Combat section later in this chapter for details on how combat works.)

Armies offer a huge advantage when attacking enemy cities. Instead suffering numerous casualties by sending in a ton of individual units, use Armies to attack cities. The defenders, even if they slightly outclass the units in your Army, can't stand up to the barrage for long.

TIP

If you've built the Military Academy Small Wonder in one of your cities, you can use the Wonder to produce Armies. That leaves you free to use your Leaders to complete the production of expensive Wonders and improvements.

COMBAT

Even if you're a pacifist, you'll deal with combat over the course of every game. Sometimes, you have to conquer one or more of your neighbors for more room, or you have to defend yourself against hostile incursion. Either way, your units are bound to clash with your opponents' troops, so it's good to know how the combat system works—and how you can make the system work for *you*.

Combat Basics

As you know, combat is initiated when a unit attempts to enter a terrain square that is occupied by an opposing unit. The percentage chance for the attacker to win is derived as follows:

(Attacker's Offensive Power)/((Attacker's Offensive Power)+(Defender's Defensive Power))=Percent chance for attacker to win

For example, a Swordsman with an Offensive Power of 3 attacks a Warrior with a Defensive Power of 1. Using the above equation, the Swordsman has a 3/(3+1), or 75 percent, chance of damaging the Warrior, leaving the Warrior with a 25 percent chance of damaging the Swordsman in each round. The defender's Defensive Power can be modified by a number of factors, as shown in table 8-5.

TABLE 8-5. DEFENSE MODIFIERS

SITUATION	DEFENSE MULTIPLIER
Defender is in a City (size 7–12)	+50%
Defender is in a Metropolis (size 13+)	+100%
Defender is in a city with Walls	+50%
Defender is in a city with a Coastal Fortress	+50%*
Defender is in a fortress	+25%
Defender is fortified	+50%
Defender is on a Forest or Jungle square	+25%
Defender is on a Hill square	+50%
Defender is on a Mountain square	+100%

* Versus naval attacks

NOTE

Defense bonuses are cumulative. For example, a Marine normally has a defense value of 8. When the unit is fortified in a fortress, its defense value is 14 (8+4+2).

After all of the bonuses are applied, the combat is resolved. Combat plays out in a series of rounds where the combat equation is applied repeatedly, with each unit losing one hit point per round. In most cases, combat ends when one unit or the other runs out of hit points.

Hit points for undamaged units in *Civilization III* are the same across the board:

- Conscript units have 2 hit points.
- Regular units have 3 hit points.
- Veteran units have 4 hit points.
- Elite units have 5 hit points.

The unit's health bar shows you its current number of hit points.

"Fast" units—units with a movement factor of 2 or higher—automatically retreat from combat when they're losing. Basically, they back out of the conflict when they're down to one hit point. This is a great tool for preserving valuable units, but only if you accede to their wisdom! If one of your units retreats from combat, move it well out of the battle zone before an enemy comes along and finishes it off!

Healing Damage

When a unit is damaged it remains damaged until it has time to heal. Units heal one hit point for every turn that they remain inactive—that is, every turn they don't move or attack. The catch is that units heal only when they're in neutral territory or within the cultural boundaries of your civilization. Move damaged units out of enemy territory as soon as they are injured. If you don't, the weakened unit is ripe for destruction.

Bypass the need to retreat for healing by building the Battlefield Medicine Small Wonder. (See chapter VII for details.)

NOTE

Even when you build Battlefield Medicine, air units based on Carriers do not heal. They must be re-based to one of your cities to repair their damage.

Air Combat

Fighters, Jet Fighters, F-15s, and Stealth Fighters—units that are capable of flying air superiority missions—are the only units that can engage in air-to-air combat. When on an air superiority mission, these units automatically engage any air unit that flies into their range. Air-to-air combat plays out in the same manner as ground combat.

Air units stationed inside cities as defenders don't gain any combat bonuses from defensive improvements.

Bombardments

Bombardments are new to *Civilization III*. Artillery units, warships, bombers, and fighters can all perform bombardment missions.

Bombardments generally don't target any specific part of a target square. Instead, they randomly hit units, improvements, fortresses, population, and so on—anything that might be in the target area. The one exception is the precision strike mission available to Stealth Bombers and Fighters. This mission allows you to target a specific city improvement.

Although they're by no means certain to take out defenders or hit vital improvements, bombardments are advisable as a precursor to any conventional attack on a well-defended city.

NOTE

Just by glancing at their statistics, you might think bombardment units—especially the land variety—are a waste. Nothing could be further from the truth. These units act as equalizers, chipping away at the hit points of vastly superior units and making them easier to take out.

Combat Strategies

Now that you know how the combat system works, you can probably formulate a number of basic combat strategies on your own—such as, don't expect a Spearman to hold off an invading platoon of Tanks. Now, let's look at a few combat tips and strategies that you might not have thought of.

Always Upgrade Your Units

This might seem like a pretty basic strategy especially now that upgrading units is so easy, but you'd be surprised how, when you get caught up in the game, you tend to forget little things like this. It's not until a neighboring civilization's invading hordes sack one of your oldest cities that you slap yourself on the head and say, "Dang! Were there still Spearmen defending that place?"

Unit upgrades become available when you discover new technologies, but the game doesn't remind you when the upgrades are available—you have to learn that on your own. Table 8-6 lists all of the upgradable units, the units to which they can be upgraded, and the civilization advances that make the upgrades possible.

TABLE 8-6. UNIT UPGRADE AVAILABILITY

UNIT	UPGRADES TO:	AFTER THE DISCOVERY OF:
Archer	Longbowman	Invention
Artillery	Radar Artillery	Robotics
Bomber	Stealth Bomber	Stealth
Bowman	Longbowman	Invention
Cannon	Artillery	Replaceable Parts
Caravel	Galleon	Magnetism
Catapult	Cannon	Metallurgy
Chariot	Horseman	Horseback Riding
Fighter	Jet Fighter	Rocketry
Galleon	Transport	Combustion
Galley	Caravel	Astronomy
Hoplite	Musketman	Gunpowder
Horseman	Knight	Chivalry
Impi	Musketman	Gunpowder
Infantry	Mech Infantry	Computers
Jaguar Warrior	Swordsman	Iron Working

continued on next page

TABLE 8-6. UNIT UPGRADE AVAILABILITY, CONTINUED

UNIT	UPGRADES TO:	AFTER THE DISCOVERY OF:
Knight	Cavalry	Military Tradition
Mounted Warrior	Knight	Chivalry
Musketeer	Rifleman	Nationalism
Musketman	Rifleman	Nationalism
Panzer	Modern Armor	Synthetic Fibers
Pikeman	Musketman	Gunpowder
Rider	Cavalry	Military Tradition
Rifleman	Infantry	Replaceable Parts
Samurai	Cavalry	Military Tradition
Spearman	Pikeman	Feudalism
Tank	Modern Armor	Synthetic Fibers
War Chariot	Knight	Chivalry
War Elephant	Cavalry	Military Tradition
Warrior	Swordsman	Iron Working

TIP

Unit upgrades are most important for your defensive units. If you can't afford to upgrade all of your units, always upgrade your city defenders first.

Deal Swiftly with Barbarians

Barbarians aren't as faceless as they once were—they're now minor tribes with names and bases of operation. Still, a Barbarian is an annoyance that must be dealt with.

Because Barbarians now arise from small villages that you can easily locate on the map, don't let them walk all over you. As soon as they start harassing one of your cities, look for their village. If you don't see it, send a solid offensive unit in the direction from which the attackers always arrive. Take a circuitous course so that you don't run into one or more of them head-on.

Eventually, you'll find their village. When you do, attack it. Barbarian villages are usually defended by only one unit, and are easy to wipe out (especially on the easier difficulty levels). This solves your Barbarian problem and nets you some Gold as well. Sacking a Barbarian village is the same as capturing a Barbarian leader in the previous *Civilization* games, only easier—the villages don't run away.

Taking Advantage of the New Zones of Control

Units no longer project a Zone of Control that prevents opposing units from moving within one terrain square of them. This is a nice feature in that it makes moving around the map in peacetime a lot easier. But, in uneasy times, it makes it easier for your opponents to move through your territory unchallenged.

Certain units in the game still project Zones of Control, but they work a little differently than they did in the previous *Civ* games. Instead of preventing enemies

from passing through, they automatically attack enemy units that pass through the Zone—*without being attacked in return*. By setting up units that project a Zone of Control at intervals along your empire's borders, you can greatly reduce an enemy's chances of getting through to your cities undamaged. When possible, place your units on terrain squares that give them a visibility and/or defensive advantage.

Setting up a Zone of Control perimeter along the border.

A list of units that project Zones of Control can be found in the Civilopedia.

The Benefits of Fortresses

Fortresses have always been one of the overlooked military advantages in *Civilization*. In *Civ III*, these already useful structures become even more effective.

Form an effective frontline defense for your cities by having your Workers construct several fortresses within your city radius and fortify several units within each.

The units receive the fortification and the fortress defensive bonuses as well as a new attack bonus. Units stationed in a fortress act as if they have a Zone of Control (as described earlier)—they attack any enemy units that pass within one square of them without being attacked in return.

For added protection, extend the fortress perimeter strategy to include fortresses along key approach paths to your empire near your empire's borders.

The Art of Paradropping

Capturing cities is the Paratrooper's specialty. Any opposing city within paradrop range is ripe for the taking and, if you're at war, don't hesitate. There are a couple of ways to take advantage of this unit's unique capabilities.

If you have the time and resources, stockpile a number of Paratroopers in your city and drop them all in the squares surrounding the target city on a single turn. On the next turn, attack the city with the Paratroopers. This strategy depends on your having enough Paratroopers to get the job done, and the losses are usually heavy if the city is well defended. (Paratroopers aren't the best offensive units available.) Bolster your attack capabilities by using a Helicopter to airdrop some stronger attack units—Marines, for instance—to help the Paratroopers.

Another method combines a conventional city siege with a paradrop. Bombard the target city with artillery units, naval units, and/or bombers (or any combination thereof) to weaken the city's defenses before you send in the Paratroopers. This usually results in fewer Paratrooper losses.

The third and most certain method should only be used if you have no intention of turning away from your warlike ways in the remainder of the game. It involves nuclear warfare, and the diplomatic consequences are always dire. But, it does work nicely.

Drop an ICBM on the target city. This has a good chance of clearing out all of the city's defenders. When the city is defenseless, drop your Paratrooper directly into the city and, voilà! It's yours! Make sure you drop in enough Paratroopers to hold the city until you can get some more powerful defenders to the site. Your hostile enemies are sure to be gunning for you when you pull this stunt.

Keeping the Good Land to Yourself

The addition of right-of-passage treaties and the elimination of traditional Zones of Control makes the peacetime world an easier place to navigate. Unfortunately, it also makes it easy for your greedy neighbors to take advantage of your hospitality and hone in on your territory by squeezing a city in among your own.

When there is a right-of-passage agreement in effect, watch your neighbors' troop movements closely. Military units are fine—they're usually just passing through on their way to smite someone else. But watch for Settlers. When you see your neighbor's Settler enter your territory, determine its course immediately. If you think the Settler is heading for a prime piece of your real estate, set up roadblocks—fortified units blocking all roads into the area and, perhaps, a couple more in the spot where you think your opponent is planning to build. It is to your advantage to keep your empire contiguous, so preventing this sort of peaceful incursion is important.

> **TIP**
>
> *If you can afford to do so—and if doing so will create a city that languishes due to lack of resources or the close proximity of other cities—the best way to cut off a neighbor's intrusive city building inside your territory is to rush your own Settler to the potential site and build a new city before your neighbor gets a chance to do so.*

Use Precision Strikes

It doesn't take long to realize that bombarding cities before you attempt to capture them is a good idea. The softer the city defenses, the easier it is to march in and take over. The only problem is that bombardment is very random—you never know what you're going to hit.

When Stealth Bombers and Fighters become available, you can use precision strikes to take out specific city improvements. This can be extremely helpful prior to an invasion. For instance, you can target a city's SAM Battery to keep your aircraft safe, or you can take out the city's Coastal Fortress to allow easier approach from the sea.

Precision strikes are useful even if you don't plan to take the city outright. By targeting happiness-inducing improvements—Cathedrals, Colosseums, and so on— you can throw the city into disorder. Or, a series of precision strikes at the enemy's science improvements— Libraries, Universities, and Research Labs— can bring their research efforts to a grinding halt, allowing you to gain an edge (or to catch up if you've fallen behind).

> **NOTE**
>
> When all of the improvements in a target city have been destroyed, precision strikes target the city's population.

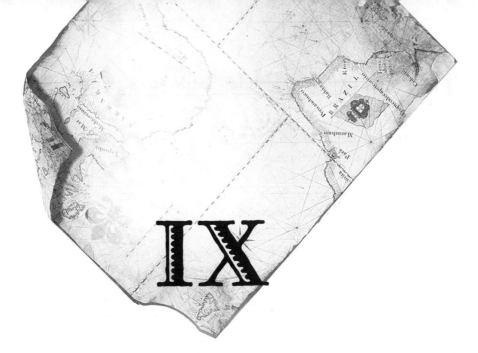

IX

THE MANY PATHS TO VICTORY

There was a time when victory in the *Civilization®* game was achieved in one of two ways—either you were the first to build a spaceship and have it reach Alpha Centauri or you completely wiped out all of your opponents. Both were challenging, and both were fun, but both were an all-or-nothing proposition.

Civilization III introduces a number of new victory conditions. You can still reach for the stars and exterminate your enemies if you want to, but you now have other options as well.

This chapter looks at the six victory conditions available in *Civ® III* and explains how to achieve them.

NOTE

If you'd rather not allow certain victory types, you can disable the ones you don't want when you're setting up a new game.

SPACE VICTORY

The space race is one of several nonconfrontational victory conditions. *Civilization* veterans are no doubt familiar with this one. While it's still one of the more difficult victories to achieve, building your starship has gotten a lot easier.

You can start building your spaceship as soon as you complete the Apollo Program Small Wonder. There are 10 spaceship components, each of which requires a different advance and/or special resource to build. You must build one (and only one) of each spaceship component to complete your spaceship and send it on its way.

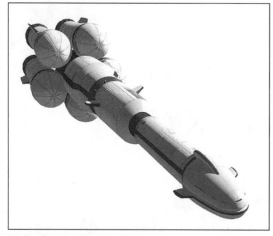

Alpha Centauri or bust!

If you're shooting for this victory condition, follow a peaceful line of research throughout the Industrial Ages and Modern Times (see chapter VI for details.) Make Space Flight your first Modern research goal. To build all the spaceship components you also need:

- The Laser
- Satellites
- Superconductor
- Synthetic Fibers

In addition, you'll need access to the following strategic resources:

- Aluminum
- Rubber
- Uranium

Here are a few additional pointers:

- **Play on a large world.** The bigger, the better. The less contact you have with other civilizations, the more time you'll have to research your way to a decisive lead.

- **Choose a science-minded civilization.** Big time science output is the key to victory here, so play as a civilization with Scientific ability. (See chapter II for details.)

- **Start the parts early.** As soon as any spaceship part becomes available, build it. The faster you build them all, the faster you'll win.

- **Protect your cities.** Losing a city that's building a spaceship part sets back your schedule. Be particularly careful to protect your capital. If the capital falls during spaceship construction, you have to start building the ship again from scratch.

NOTE

Good news! You no longer have to wait for your spaceship to reach Alpha Centauri. If you complete and launch the ship before any of the other civilizations, you immediately win!

CONQUEST VICTORY

Sometimes, nothing beats a good old-fashioned war—or, endless centuries thereof—to prove that you're the superior leader. Of all of the victory conditions available, the conquest victory is the most challenging in terms of resources and population happiness. Turn after turn of pumping out military units taxes your shield production to the limit, and fielding all of those units makes it difficult to keep war weariness at bay.

Here are a few general tips for you warmonger types:

- **Choose a small world.** If you intend to conquer the world, don't prolong things by starting out halfway across the map from your neighbors. Small worlds bring things to a head quickly.

- **Select the right civilization.** Play a civilization that has a military edge. If you like to conquer early, try the Japanese or the Chinese (Samurai and Riders). For late-game fighting, go with the Germans (Panzers rule the Industrial Ages).

- **Start early.** Regardless of which civilization you play, seek out your neighbors early. Take out your weakest enemies before their empires have time to spread.

- **Build military improvements and Wonders.** A Barracks in every city is a must. Build Wonders such as Battlefield Medicine, Military Academy, and any others that give you an edge over your rivals.

- **Build any and all "happiness generators."** Because of the war weariness you're bound to experience, make sure all of your cities have Temples, Cathedrals, and Police Stations. Make happiness Wonders high on your priority list.

- **Be ruthless.** Make friends with your neighbors for your own selfish reasons. Bring the enemy to his knees, accept his offer of tribute, sign the treaty, and *then* wipe him out when his Gold is in your coffers.

CULTURAL VICTORY

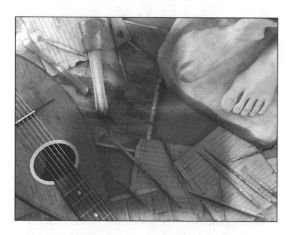

Culture is a new concept, but not a particularly difficult one to grasp. You can see your Culture grow throughout the game as you build Culture-producing improvements and Wonders in your cities. This expands your borders throughout the game and often leads to the defection of awed neighboring cities from their culturally poor motherlands to your burgeoning paradise.

If you're feeling up to the challenge, you can actually win the game by building the end-all, be-all Cultural Mecca of the world. To do this, you must achieve one of two goals:

- Build up a single city with a Culture Point value of 20,000 or more.

- Build your entire civilization's Culture Point value to 80,000 and have that total be at least twice as high as your closest rival.

> **NOTE**
>
> Obviously, these point totals refer to an accumulation of Culture Points over the course of the game and *not* to the number of Culture Points earned in a single turn.

Here are some tips for achieving a Cultural Victory:

- **Choose a Culture-friendly civilization.** Because Culture Points are generated by religious and scientific improvements, play as a civilization that has one of these specialties.

- **Build *everything* that generates Culture.** This one's a no-brainer. The more Culture-producing units and Wonders you build, the more Culture points you earn. (Culture is discussed in detail in chapter IV.)

- **Spread your Culture over many cities.** Yes, you can win a Cultural Victory by building up a single city to super-Culture status, but that's dangerous. If the city is captured, there go your victory plans. If you spread the Culture, the loss of one or two cities won't be as big a deal.

- **Protect your assets.** Protect your culturally rich cities. If you *do* try the one-city method, make sure that city has an airtight defense.

DIPLOMATIC VICTORY

After someone builds the United Nations Wonder, there are periodic votes to elect the new UN leader. If you're elected, you win the game! It sounds easy, but it isn't. To be eligible for the post, you must meet one of the following criteria:

- Be the one who builds the United Nations Wonder

- Control at least 25 percent of the world's territory

- Control at least 25 percent of the world's population

There are always at least two candidates put up for election. If two candidates aren't eligible, the second candidate is the civilization with the largest population.

When the election takes place, you must win the majority of the votes from other civilizations.

This is, perhaps, the most difficult victory to achieve. For the most part, play the game as if attempting a Space or Cultural Victory—in other words, take the peaceful route. In addition, keep the following in mind:

- **Build the United Nations.** This is a sure way to become eligible for the vote, so why leave it to chance if this is the victory path you've chosen?

- **Keep your diplomatic slate clean.** If you want the others to vote for you, play fair and square when it comes to negotiations. No breaking treaties, making harsh demands, and so on. Getting along with your neighbors is the key to a Diplomatic victory.

- **Do a little brown-nosing.** Don't wait for your neighbors to come to you. Go to them from time to time and initiate negotiations. Offer them small tokens of your esteem—a few Gold here, a map there—and ask for nothing in return. This helps to maintain good will.

- **Don't play favorites.** Do your best to be everyone's friend. When they ask you to take sides against someone, counter-offer with a right-of-passage treaty that allows them to conduct their war without your direct involvement.

For details on the finer points of diplomacy, see chapter V.

DOMINATION VICTORY

The nice thing about the Domination Victory is that it can work for two totally opposite gameplay styles. To win in this manner, you must have at least 66 percent of the world's land surface within your empire's borders (water doesn't count).

You can follow one of two paths to Domination. If you like the military approach, follow the advice given for the Conquest Victory. By rolling in and capturing enemy cities (or by wiping out enemy civilizations and building your own cities in their former territory), you can slowly but surely spread your empire's influence over the requisite amount of the world.

The second Domination method follows the Cultural Victory route. By building up your Culture and spreading it around about equally in all of your cities, you cause your empire's borders to grow. By combining the strategies for Cultural Victory with peaceful but steady expansion throughout the game, you can achieve the Domination Victory without resorting to undue violence.

TIP

For a fast Domination game, don't play on a large world. Domination Victory method can be achieved more rapidly on small worlds with limited landmass.

HISTOGRAPHIC VICTORY

The final victory relies on that old standby, your Civilization Score. Throughout the game, your score is constantly tracked. You receive points each turn based on a number of factors, including:

- The amount of territory in your empire
- The number of happy citizens in your cities
- The state of your relations with your neighbors

If the game ends before any of the other five victory conditions has been achieved—if you retire in mid-game, for instance—the player with the highest average score over the course of the game wins. It's that simple.

To be assured of a Histographic Victory, just pick a strategy for one of the five other victory types and stick to it. Your odds of winning a Histographic Victory are better if you follow a peaceful strategy, however, because your population tends to stay happier when you're not at war.

NOTE

A Histographic Victory is not one that you usually try for from the start—it's just a sort of consolation prize for doing your best up to the time you retire.

THE EDITOR IN THE
CIVILIZATION® *III* GAME

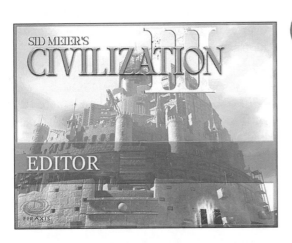

ne of the best things about the *Civilization*® *II* game was that it was infinitely expandable and customizable. The built-in editor let you build maps to your heart's content, and the brilliant use of the infamous *rules.txt* file allowed would-be designers to modify the game. If they were really ambitious, they could create scenarios of their own simply by editing the text file and, perhaps, altering a few graphics files.

Civilization III one-ups its predecessor by including Civ3Edit—a full-featured editor that eliminates the need to fiddle with text files. Now you can draw maps and edit just about every game feature in a single, simple-to-use application. To start

the editor, go to the installed directory of your game and double-click the Civ3Edit application icon.

This final chapter provides a basic overview of this powerful editing tool.

CREATING MAPS

Civ3Edit follows the conventions of most popular computer art programs. If you've ever used Paint (the drawing program included with Windows), then basic map building will be a snap.

NOTE

You also can create a random map by selecting Generate Map from the Map menu. Then modify the map using the techniques described in the following sections.

World Size and Base Terrain Type

You start off with a blank "normal" world map that consists entirely of Ocean terrain. Start by setting the world size that you want. To change the world size, go to the Map menu and select Clear Map. This brings up the Clear Map window. Select the world size you want from the drop-down menu.

You can also change the base terrain type. This is the terrain that covers the entire map when the blank map is created. Ocean usually works best, but you can start out with any terrain type you like.

Once you've set both to your liking, click OK to continue.

Building the Terrain

To draw terrain on your map, move the cursor to the spot where you want the terrain to appear and click. By default, the terrain you start drawing with is Desert. Every time you click, a new Desert square appears. To change the type of terrain you're drawing with, open the Map menu and choose Select Brush Type. When the Select Terrain Type window appears, choose the terrain you want from the drop-down menu.

To draw multiple terrain squares, click and hold the button and drag the cursor across the screen. This creates an interconnected series of terrain squares. To cover a broader area in each stroke, change the brush size by opening the Map menu and selecting one of the four brush options from the Terrain Brush Size options.

To change an existing terrain square to a different type, select the desired terrain type as described earlier and click the square you want to change.

Adding Special Features to the Map

When you have your basic terrain laid out, start adding special features to the map. Open the Map menu and highlight Select Brush Type. Besides the normal Terrain types, you also can select the following:

- **Good:** Selecting this option brings up the Goods window, which allows you to select any of the special resources in the game—Gold, Horses, Iron, Silk, and so on. (See chapter III for info on the effects of special resources.) Select the Good you want to add to the map from the drop-down menu, click OK, then click the map square where you want the resource to appear.

- **Overlay:** This option allows you to add special features to the map such as terrain improvements (roads, railroads, irrigation, and so on), Barbarian encampments, pollution, "goodie huts," rivers, and even the starting positions for civilizations. Select the Overlay feature you want to add to the map from the drop-down menu, click OK, then click the map square where you want the feature to appear.

NOTE

You can place Goods and Overlays only on terrain types where they can actually appear in the game. For example, Horses can be placed only on Grasslands, Plains, and Hills, and Player Starting Locations cannot be placed on Coast, Sea, or Ocean squares. See chapter III for information on the terrain types where special resources occur in the game.

Finishing Touches and Mapmaking Tips

The new world

After you've got your map the way you want it, save it by selecting the Save option on the File menu. Save all of your map files in the *Maps* folder of the directory where the game is installed. Load your saved maps by selecting Load Map from the main menu.

Here are a few final tips to assist you in your cartographic efforts:

- **Make sure your maps have a good balance of land and sea squares.** Maps with too much land or too much water can cause the game to behave unpredictably.

- **Try to create a balanced mix of terrain.** Maps that are too hostile make the game unbelievably difficult (and perhaps impossible) to win. For example, creating a world where the land consisted of nothing but Mountains would be bad.

- **Learn by example.** Use the Generate Map option to create a few random maps and examine the layout the game uses when creating a world. The maps created by the game are designed to provide an environment that lends itself to fun, balanced gameplay.

EDITING THE RULES

The Edit Rules option on the Rules menu accesses the most powerful feature of Civ3Edit. From the Edit Rules window you can change just about any rule, feature, name, and statistic in *Civilization III*.

The Edit Rules window is divided into 19 categories. Access a section by clicking on its tab at the top of the window. Also access each individual section by selecting it from the drop-down Edit menu on the main screen.

The following sections briefly describe the rules categories and the options that you can edit on each.

Citizens

This window allows you to edit the designations and characteristics of the citizens that appear in all of your cities. The available options are:

- **Citizen Type:** The type of citizen (Laborer, Entertainer, Tax Collector, or Scientist). You can change these names by clicking the Rename button.

- **Plural Name:** The pluralized version of the citizen type. Example: "Laborers."

- **Default Citizen:** The type of citizen that appears each time a city grows. Laborer is the normal default. Setting this to one of the other citizen types would wreak havoc in your cities.

- **Prerequisite:** Allows you to set an advance prerequisite for each citizen type *except* the Default Citizen type.

- **Bonuses:** The additional luxuries, research (science), and/or taxes each citizen of this type provides. (Example: Tax Collectors provide a bonus of one tax.)

> **NOTE**
>
> Many of the editor sections contain an option called "Civilopedia Entry." This is the category and name by which the game references the item in question. In most cases, this entry should not be altered.

Civilizations

This set of options allows you to set the characteristics and priorities of each of the 16 civilizations in the game. Available options allow you to change all of the characteristics you can change when customizing a civilization during game setup (see the game manual for details). In addition, the following options are available:

- **Personality:** In this section, you can set the civilization's preferred form of government, a government that they always avoid, and their level of aggression.

- **Animations:** Sets the animations associated with changing research eras. *Don't change these settings!*

- **Culture Group:** Sets the civilization's global culture (see chapter V for details on this characteristic).

- **City Names:** The list of default city names for the civilization. The names are used in order from top to bottom throughout the game.

- **Great Leaders:** The list of names for the Great Leaders who appear for this civilization.

- **Team Colors:** The accent color used for the civilization's units.

- **Bonuses:** Allows you to set the civ-specific advantage types for this civilization. Normally, each civilization has two (see chapter II, table 2-1), but you can select all six if you like.

- **Free Techs:** The advances the civilization has at the start of the game. Normally, each civilization starts with two (see chapter II, table 2-2) but you can select up to four.

- **Governor:** The AI equivalent of the City Governor (see chapter IV), which sets the city management priorities for the civilization. You can select any or all of the available priority options.

Civilization Advances

This portion of the editor allows you to alter the characteristics of the civilization advances. Besides the ability to rename the advances, the following options are available:

- **Icon:** Changes the Civilopedia and research tree icon that identifies the advance.

- **Cost:** The number of accumulated science icons it takes to discover the advance.

- **X: and Y:** The screen coordinates of the advance as it appears on the research tree. Under most circumstances, don't alter these numbers.

- **Era:** The era in which the advance is available. You can switch eras without causing game problems (in most cases) but doing so might cause art oddities on the research tree.

- **Prerequisites:** The other advances that must be researched in order to research this advance. You can set up to four prerequisites. Be careful not to set impossible prerequisites. For example, don't set Medicine as the prerequisite for Sanitation if you've already set Sanitation as the prerequisite for Medicine.

- **Flags:** Here you set the many characteristics of the advance, such as its effects on cities, improvements, and units, its effect on trade, and whether or not the advance is required in order to move on to the next research era.

Combat Experience

This window accesses the hit point information for your units. Here, you can change the base hit point values for each of the four unit experience levels—Conscript, Regular, Veteran, and Elite. You also can rename the experience levels.

Culture

This window allows you to set the Culture Point ratios that affect your opponents' perception of you throughout the game, and the effects of these ratios on propaganda attempts by spies. (See chapter V, tables 5-4, 5-6, and 5-7 for details on what these settings mean.)

Difficulty Levels

Here you change the names of the various difficulty levels available and set the number of citizens at each level that are "born" content. The more citizens born content, the easier it is to maintain happiness in your cities.

Diplomats and Spies

The options here allow you to change the menu designations for diplomat and spy activities and assign each activity as a function of either a diplomat or a spy or both.

For example, here you could change the Steal Plans mission from a spy function to a diplomat function. By doing so, you wouldn't need to plant a spy in your embassy to perform this mission.

Eras

This window allows you to rename the four eras of the game—Ancient Times, Middle Ages, Industrial Ages, and Modern Times—and set the naming conventions used to identify your researchers when the discovery of an advance is announced. (Example: "Roman Mystics have discovered....")

General Settings

General Settings is a catchall screen with a huge number of miscellaneous global game options. The options include:

- **Road Movement:** The movement multiplier for ground units moving along a road.

- **Food and Gold:** Allows you to set the amount of food consumed by each citizen per turn and the amount of Gold in your starting treasury.

- **Corruption:** The number of cities you can have before corruption starts to rise exponentially. (The actual level of corruption is still dependent on your type of government.)

- **Wealth:** Sets the base exchange rate of shields to Gold for cities "building" Wealth. (A setting of "8" means that the exchange rate is 8 shields = 1 Gold.) This rate is halved after the discovery of Economics.

- **Hurry Production:** Sets the exchange rate of Gold (or citizens) to shields when rushing a production job.

- **Citizen Mood:** Allows you to set a variety of options concerning citizen mood and related topics, such as the turn penalties between conscriptions and sacrificing citizens for rush jobs.

- **Culture:** These options are currently not used in the game.

- **Various Unit Abilities:** Allows you to set options such as the benefit you reap from harvesting forests, number of cities needed for armies, and air attack intercept probabilities.

- **City Size Levels:** Allows you to rename the three city sizes (Town, City, and Metropolis) and edit the size at which Towns and Cities grow to the next level.

- **Culture Levels:** Change the wording used to describe Culture levels at each stage of their development. You also can set the number of Culture Points needed to advance to the next level. (This doesn't affect your actual Culture Points or the total number needed to win a Cultural victory.)

- **Defensive Bonuses:** Lets you set the defensive bonus percentage added for various factors, including city size, fortresses, rivers, fortified units, and so on.

- **Spaceship Parts:** Lets you set the number of spaceship parts (and the quantities of each part) you need to build to achieve a Space Victory.

- **Default Units:** Allows you to change a variety of default unit types, including default Barbarian land and sea units and civilization starting units. The most potent option is the Battle-Created Unit (normally a Leader), which you can set to any unit in the game—including an Army!

- **Default Money Resource:** The special resource that appears on the terrain square when you visit a "goodie hut" that gives you Gold.

Governments

This window allows you to manipulate the characteristics of the six government types. Besides being able to rename each government, the following characteristics can be changed:

- **Prerequisite:** The advance that must be discovered before you can switch to this government type. (Not available for governments flagged as Transition Type or Default Type.)

- **Corruption and Waste:** Allows you to set the level of corruption and waste under the government type. Minimal is the lowest and Catastrophic is the highest. Communal sets the same level of corruption and waste in each city.

(See chapter V for details on corruption and waste.)

- **Unit Support Costs:** Allows you to set the amount of Gold paid each turn to support units and the number of support-free units per Town/City/Metropolis.

- **Rate Cap:** Allows you to set an upper percentage limit on the amount of commerce that can be allocated to science. Multiply this number by 10 to obtain the percentage. (So, a Rate Cap of "10" means you can set science to 100 percent.)

- **Worker Rate:** The relative rate at which Workers perform their tasks. For example, Anarchy has a Work Rate of "1" and Democracy has a Work Rate of "3." Workers in a Democracy perform their tasks three times as fast as workers in an Anarchy.

- **Assimilation Chance:** The base percentage chance that a city under this government type will voluntarily defect to a neighboring civilization.

- **Draft Limit:** The number of citizens per city you can turn into military units.

- **Military Police Limit:** The maximum number of military units that can be garrisoned in a city to impose martial law (one unhappy citizen is made content by each).

- **Resistance Modifier Vs.:** The numeric multiplier that determines the resistance level of captured cities based on the type of government that controlled them at the time of the capture. Captured cities tend to put up less resistance if the conquering civilization's government is more advanced than theirs.

- **Hurrying Production:** Changes how you speed the completion of units and improvements. Choose from Cannot Hurry, Forced Labor (population loss), or Paid Labor (pay Gold to complete the project).

- **War Weariness:** Sets the effects of war weariness for the government type. Low is the equivalent of Republic and High is the equivalent of Democracy.

- **Espionage:** Allows you to set the experience level of diplomats and spies (the more experienced they are, the better their chance of completing missions). You can also select one diplomatic/spy mission to which the government is immune and the bribery (propaganda) resistance multiplier for the government versus all other government types.

- **Flags:** Allows you to set certain general characteristics of the government, such as whether it's the transition government (the one that you switch to when you change governments) or the default government (the one you start the game with).

- **Great Person Mood Modifiers:** This is not currently used in the game.

- **Ruler Titles:** Allows you to change the titles by which you are addressed under this government.

Improvements and Wonders

This section of the editor allows you to edit every aspect of the improvements, Wonders of the World, and Small Wonders. You can change a multitude of characteristics.

NOTE

The options here are too numerous to list individually. To get an idea of what each option and ability does, scroll through the building list and compare the statistics in the editor to the building's stats and description in chapter VII to get an idea of what each setting indicates.

- **Required:** Allows you to set the advance, building, or government type required for the construction of the improvement/Wonder.

- **Required Resources:** Allows you to set up to two different strategic resources required to produce the building.

- **Happy/Unhappy Faces:** Allows you to set the building's effects on the city's populace. For example, setting Unhappy to "1" means that the building makes one unhappy citizen content. The "(all cities)" setting spreads the effects over all of your cities rather than just the city where the improvement/Wonder is built.

- **Other Characteristics:** Allows you to set restrictions on the location of the building, its category, and the scope of its effects. For example, a "Coastal installation" can only be built in coastal cities, and "Continental mood effects" restricts the effect on citizens to the continent where the building is built.

- **Num. Req. Bldgs.:** Sets the number of prerequisite buildings (specified under Prerequisites) required to produce the building. For example, Battlefield Medicine requires five Hospitals.

- **Category:** The type of building— improvement, Wonder, or Small Wonder. The category determines the options and effects available for the building.

- **Cost:** The number of shields it takes to produce the building.

- **Maintenance:** The amount of Gold you must pay each turn to maintain the building.

- **Culture:** The number of Culture Points the building generates each turn.

- **Production:** The number of extra shields each city square produces when the building is present.

- **Pollution:** The number of pollution points produced by the building each turn.

- **Description:** The Civilopedia description of the building.

- **Spaceship Part Type:** The type of space-ship part the building emulates (1–10).

- **Combat Values:** Allows you to set the combat modifiers the building imparts to its city in an attack.

- **Improvements:** The specific benefits an improvement provides to its city, and the unique abilities and characteristics of the building.

- **Wonders:** The settings for Wonder-specific abilities, including the advance that makes the Wonder obsolete, the Wonder's happiness effects on other buildings, the building the Wonder emulates in every city (or in every city on its continent), and the specific effects associated with the Wonder.

- **Small Wonders:** The specific effects associated with Small Wonders.

Natural Resources

Here you can edit all of the characteristics of the special resources in the game. The available options are:

- **Icon:** The map image used for the resource. Changing this number causes the game to reference a different image. For example, changing the Horses icon from "0" to "1" makes Horses appear as Iron on the map.

- **Farm Bonuses:** The additional food, shields, and/or commerce produced by the terrain when the resource is present.

- **Type:** Identifies the resource as a bonus resource (a nontradable special resource, such as Gold); a luxury resource

(a happiness-inducing special resource such as Silk); or a strategic resource (a resource required for certain improvements/Wonders, such as Iron).

- **Prerequisite:** The advance that must be discovered before the resource appears on the map. For example, Horses don't appear until you discover Horseback Riding.

- **Appearance Ratio:** The ratio of luxury and strategic resource squares to the number of civilizations in the game. Setting this to 100 means that a six-civilization game would have six terrain squares with each luxury/strategic resource, 200 would mean 12 each, and so on. (Setting this to "0" picks a random number between 50 and 100.)

- **Disappearance Probability:** Sets the likelihood of the resource disappearing (being depleted) each turn when it is connected to a civilization's trade network. For example, a setting of 100 means there's a 1 in 100 chance of the resource disappearing every turn. A "0" here means that the resource is never depleted.

Terrain

This portion of the editor allows you to change the rules regarding the basic terrain types. The statistics you can alter include:

- **Tile Values:** Allows you to set the base food, shield, and commerce output of the terrain.

- **Movement Cost:** The number of movement points a unit must expend to enter a terrain square of this type.

- **Defense Bonus:** The percentage modifier applied to a unit that is attacked on this terrain type.

- **Worker Job:** Allows you to set a special Worker job that can be performed on this terrain (above and beyond the jobs normally available on the terrain type in question). For example, using this setting you could allow Workers to irrigate Mountains.

- **Pollution Effect:** The type of terrain this terrain changes to when affected by global warming.

- **Possible Resources:** The types of special resources that can occur on the terrain type. (Select as many as you want for each terrain type by holding Ctrl and clicking each resource.)

Units

This set of options allows you to customize the abilities of the game's units. Besides the ability to change each unit's name, the following options are available:

- **Icon:** Changes the icon used by the unit.

- **Required:** The advance you must discover to build the unit. Don't set a prerequisite for Settlers. You can't build cities without Settlers, and you can't perform research without cities.

- **Shield Cost:** The number of shields it costs to produce the unit.

- **Pop. Cost:** The number of population points lost from a city when it produces the unit. (Example: Settlers cost two population points plus their shield cost.)

- **Moves:** The unit's base movement rate.

- **Trans. Capacity:** The number of other units the unit can transport.

- **Zone of Control:** Endows the unit with a Zone of Control. Units so endowed automatically attack enemy units that pass within one square of them (unless the opposing units are immune to Zones of Control).

- **Attack Str.:** The unit's attack factor.

- **Defense Str.:** The unit's base defensive strength.

- **Operational Range:** The operational range (applies to air units).

- **Bombard Str.:** The unit's bombardment strength.

- **Bombard Range:** The range at which the unit can launch a bombardment attack.

- **Rate of Fire:** The number of volleys fired by per bombardment.

- **Required Resources:** The strategic resources required to build the unit (choose up to three).

- **Unit Abilities:** The special abilities the unit possesses (such as nuclear weapon, amphibious capabilities, ignores Zones of Control, and so on). Select as many abilities as you like by holding Ctrl and clicking the desired items. Overloading a unit with conflicting characteristics can create unpredictable results.

- **Available to:** Allows you to restrict the unit's availability to the civilizations you select.

- **Class:** Identifies the unit as a ground, naval, or air unit and endows it with the basic characteristics of the selected class. Changing the class of pivotal units (such as Settlers and Workers) can cause unplayable situations.

- **AI Strategies:** This group of options defines how the AI uses the unit. The choices are restricted based on the unit's Class, the options selected under Unit Abilities, and certain Special Actions selections. Deselecting all AI Strategies for a unit causes the AI not to use the unit at all—which can produce unpredictable results depending on the unit.

- **Standard Orders:** Allows you to set which of the standard gameplay functions (Skip Turn, Wait, and so on) the unit is able to perform.

- **Special Actions:** Sets the special abilities the unit is able to perform. Selecting contradictory abilities—such as Finish Improvement for a Cruise Missile, for instance—can lead to unpredictable unit behavior, especially when under AI control.

- **Worker/Engineer Actions:** Allows you to assign Worker abilities and commands to a unit. Again, these features can cause odd behavior when assigned to certain units.

- **Air Missions:** Selects the air missions the unit is capable of performing. The same warning stands—oddities might result from when these attributes are assigned to units that they weren't designed for.

Unit Abilities/Unit Actions/Unit Orders

These three editor categories allow you to change the names of unit abilities (Wheeled, Ignore Zones of Control, All Terrain As Roads), unit actions (Hold, Wait, Fortify) and unit orders (Build Fortress, Build Road). This changes their verbiage in the game—nothing more. You can enter a short description of abilities and actions.

Worker Jobs

This portion of the editor deals specifically with the tasks performed by Workers—mining, building roads, and so on. In addition to the ability to change the name of each task, you can alter the following:

- **Required:** The advance you must discover before the Worker can perform the task.

- **Required Resources:** The strategic resources you must have access to for the Worker to perform the job. (You can select two.)

- **Turns to Complete:** The base number of turns required for the Worker to complete the job.

World Sizes

The final editor section allows you to manipulate a number of features regarding world size. As with many other features, you can rename the world size classifications if you wish. You also can set the following:

- **Width and Height:** The width and height of the map (as measured in terrain squares). You can set each to any value from 16 to 256.

- **Number of Civs:** The default number of civilizations included in the game for the selected world size. (You can change this manually during game setup.) Setting a high number of civilizations on a very small map can lead to unpredictable results.

- **Distance Between Civs:** The minimum distance (in map squares) between civilization starting positions. Make sure this number is set lower than the Width and Height numbers. Setting this number extremely low can lead to a very odd game.

- **Description:** Allows you to enter a brief description for the world size.

CONVERSING WITH THE CREATOR

Sid Meier has been making computer games since—well, pretty much since the *inception* of the computer game industry! With more than a dozen hit games under his belt, it's safe to say that no one knows the industry quite as well as Sid. What he has to say about game design could probably fill an entire book. So, because *this* book is about the *Civilization® III* game, we ran some questions by the legend himself and asked him for some of his thoughts on his latest creation.

Prima: *Why did you decide to do another* Civilization? *Haven't you given people enough sleepless nights?*

Sid: It was time! :) Between the tremendous amount of feedback we've had from *Civ®* players over the years and the multitude of ideas our development team had, we knew we could take the *Civ* experience to the next level...and we have!

Prima: *There are tons of* Civilization *fan sites out there, and we're sure you get lots of fan mail from avid players. How much was the* Civ III *design influenced by the suggestions and comments of existing* Civ *players?*

Sid: As I just mentioned, we've had lots of *Civ* player feedback over the years that has definitely helped us shape *Civ III*. We're very thankful to the *Civ* community for sharing their thoughts with us.

Prima: *How did your experience with* Sid Meier's Alpha Centauri *influence the design of* Civ III? *There are some obvious similarities between the two games.*

Sid: We learned a lot of good things with *Alpha Centauri*...one of which is that more does not always mean better. We took some of the cool features and technological advances we made in *SMAC* and implemented them in *Civ III*.

Prima: *There are some notable* Civ II *items—advances, units, improvements, etc.—missing from* Civilization III. *In fact, in some ways,* Civ III *seems closer in design to the original game. Was this your intention and, if so, why?*

Sid: Our goal with *Civ III* has been to take the light-hearted, fun elements of the original *Civ*, the depth of *Civ II*, and refine and improve them to add the many new features and ideas we've developed, making *Civ III* the best *Civ* experience ever.

Prima: *What happened to Fundamentalism? Some of the more militant* Civ II *players swear by it.*

Sid: It created a balance problem in the game that we couldn't rectify, so we didn't include it.

Prima: *Another interesting change is the fact that you no longer have to wait for the spaceship to reach Alpha Centauri. What prompted that change?*

Sid: We want you to be able to revel in your victory immediately!

Prima: *Both the naval and the air units work differently in* Civ III—*they operate more realistically. Did bombardment and the new air rules create any balance problems?*

Sid: In some way, every element creates a balance problem, so a major focus for us is to do what it takes to keep everything balanced. Bombardment and the new air rules did create a balance challenge, but nothing major.

Prima: *In* Civ II *Multiplayer, you were able to trade units with other civilizations.* Civ III *allows many items to be traded, but not units. Any particular reason?*

Sid: In *Civ III*, along with the multitude of things that can be traded, you can also trade Worker units.

Prima: *The idea of national borders—rather than a loose collection of city states—is an excellent addition to the game, though it tends to greatly change the player's interaction with the other civilizations. How did that idea come about, and how hard was it to integrate and balance?*

Sid: Some things are just obviously good ideas. This was one of them. However, the way in which they function based on Culture was a "breakthrough" for us. We spent a long time trying various strategies for national boundaries growing naturally. We had the idea of Culture growing out of cities and we had the desire for national boundaries. The breakthrough was when we decided that the two should be combined.

Prima: *Elvis seems to have left the building. Many players actually called the Entertainers "Elvis." Why do away with The King?*

Sid: It was time to say goodbye…and he refused to get off my blue suede shoes, so he had to go. ;-)

Prima: *What made you decide to do away with the previous trade system?*

Sid: We had some better ideas! We're really excited about the expanded trade system. A big change is that trade has been abstracted to the diplomacy system and trade advisors will no longer require you to use Caravan units. Trade goods are composed of luxuries and resources. Luxuries are goods that improve the happiness of your cities. Resources are needed to make certain military units (Iron, for example, is needed to make the Swordsman or Roman Legion units).

Prima: *In today's market, there seems to be an unwritten demand for multiplayer in every product. Do you believe that turn-based games like* Civilization *are conducive to multiplayer? In your opinion, is it still okay to make single-player-only games?*

Sid: The single-player experience has always been the main focus of *Civilization*. However, we're working on some cool multiplayer concepts that will take a fresh approach to the challenge of making multiplayer for a turned-based game fun. We're not yet ready to give details, but stay tuned.

Prima: *Was there any concept or feature that you tried to work into Civ III that just didn't work?*

Sid: We had an idea for Great People (Artists, Scientist, Politicians) in addition to Great Leaders. There was a system for defection to other countries, kidnapping, and so on. We couldn't get this to work in a satisfactory way, so we didn't include it.

Prima: *Scenarios kept* Civ II *going strong for years after its release. Are there any scenario packs planned for* Civ III*? Do you have any scenario ideas you'd like to share with us?*

Sid: The mod community is very important to us and we're dedicated to supporting them after the release of *Civ III*. Stay tuned for more details. :)

Prima: *Half the people reading this probably want to be game designers. Can you help them learn from your mistakes? Over your whole career, what mistake did you learn the most from, and what did you learn?*

Sid: I've learned to recognize when something in the game design isn't working and change it—even if that means taking a whole new approach to the game. So, I guess the lesson for young game designers is to be open to making adjustments—even big ones—if you're finding that the game just isn't working well.

Prima: *What games do you play to learn from? For fun?*

Sid: I don't really make that distinction. I like to play good games that are fun and teach you something at the same time.

Prima: *One final question.* Civilization IV. *Have you thought whether you'd like to do* Civ IV *and, if so, what it might be like?*

Sid: That's a good question. If the fans still want more after *Civ III*, then we'll talk about giving them more. :)

INDEX